BUD'S JACKET

BUD'S JACKET

AN AMERICAN FLYER EVADES THE NAZIS
IN OCCUPIED FRANCE

BY BARBARA WOJCIK
WITH JIM WOJCIK

4 square
books

The song My Buddy is reproduced on pages 155–156 with permission:
Lyrics by Gus Kahn, Music by Walter Donaldson
Copyright ©1922 (Renewed) Gilbert Keyes Music and Donaldson Publishing Co.
Canadian Rights controlled by WC Music Corp.
All rights reserved
Used by permission of Alfred Music

ISBN: 978-1-61766-288-1

Cover design by Lillian Wojcik.

Published 2020 by Chris Fayers under the imprint of
4 Square Books
Stillwater, Minnesota
maenadest@protonmail.com

Printed in the United States of America

Dedicated to:

The known and unknown French Helpers of WWII

Contents

Foreword

White Bear Lake, Minnesota
May 2015

My neighborhood book club was discussing *The Nightingale* by Kristin Hannah, then a recently-published World War II novel about two heroic sisters working for the French Resistance. At the center was an Allied airman's struggle to evade capture in occupied France.

"That part about escaping the Nazis on foot over the Pyrenees," scoffed one of the other club members. "Just too ridiculous. She must have made all that up."

"No, that really did happen," I said. "And, believe it or not, it happened to my uncle!"

My friend's doubt sparked dim memories of a phone call with my father when I first heard about Uncle Bud's wartime experiences. It was an interesting piece of family history, but in 1983, I was busy taking care of my job and family and I'm sorry to say I soon forgot all about Bud and his story.

However, some three decades later, after our book club discussion, I was curious to find out more. I knew Uncle Bud Wilschke was married to my dad's sister, Rosemary, so I decided to reach out to my cousin Jim, Bud and Rosemary's oldest son. This felt tricky. Our families had never been close. But my curiosity won out and I made the phone call.

Jim was glad to hear from me and eager to have help sorting through his dad's mementos and documents. He soon began sending emails with fascinating scans of photos and artifacts. He invited me to his house in suburban Chicago and loaned me an incredible trove of photos, letters, newspaper clippings and other memorabilia that had been stored in his basement.

With these materials, I began piecing together Bud's remarkable story. The project has been a wonderful gift to me and I am honored to work on it. Not only has the quest provided a fascinating research

May to November, 1943 Flight path and Evasion route: – – – – ➔

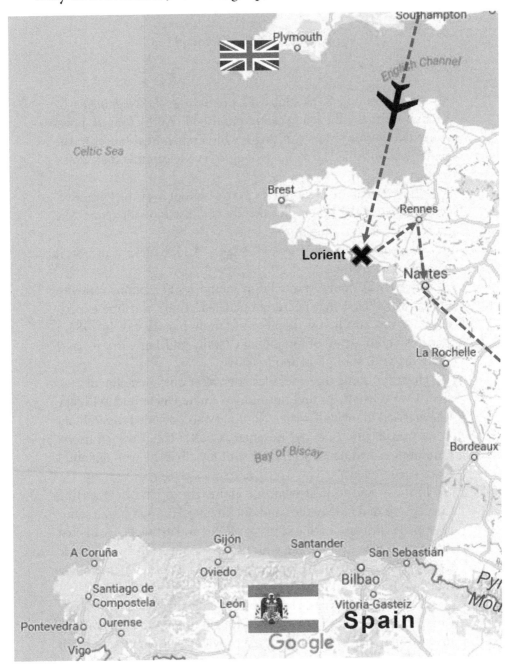

project, but on a personal level it has reconnected my cousin's family with mine.

Like many World War II veterans, Bud Wilschke rarely spoke of his wartime experiences. He didn't seem to talk a lot about other topics either so I had just a few impressions of the person I was to learn so much about. All I remembered of him was an 'uncle,' a kind, calm and devoted family man.

But 30 years ago in that phone conversation, my dad had foreshadowed what I was to learn.

"Uncle Bud," he said, "has quite a story to tell."

Bud's personal collection.

Prologue

Jim Wilschke Jr. had been rummaging in his parents' closets for 30 minutes but he was still coming up empty. Escaping the soggy Chicago spring, he had been visiting the Mount Dora, Florida, home of his mom and dad, Bud and Rosemary Crandell Wilschke, for a week. Around the dinner table with his parents, he would often ask them for stories about their lives when they were young. Now he was thinking about his dad's World War II flying jacket. Bud remembered seeing it and playing with it when he was a boy, admiring its tough leather and soft fleece, fascinated by its many pockets. It was mysterious, manly, and inspiring. Where was it?

His parents had moved from Chicago to Mount Dora in the early 1980s after Jim Sr. ("Bud") retired from his career as a lineman for Illinois Bell Telephone Co., his steady employer for over 35 years. Now in their late 70s and after a lifetime of smoking Pall Malls and Marlboros, Bud and Rosemary were both in fragile health.

Jim found Bud reclining in his favorite chair.

"Dad? Hey, Dad? Oh, sorry. Are you napping?"

The old soldier slowly opened his eyes.

"Do you know where your Air Force flying jacket is?"

"Let me think." Bud paused for a moment to consider the possibilities. "I guess Bill has it."

"Why does Uncle Bill have your jacket?"

"Truth is, he doesn't actually *have* it. He gave it to the local Boy Scout troop. They had a project going on about World War II and the Invasion of Europe and so we let 'em have it."

"What?! DAD?! We need to get that back now. I'll call Uncle Bill."

"Why?" Bud reached for a cigarette from the big red pack on the table next to the recliner.

"What's the big deal about the jacket all of a sudden? I wasn't using it right now. Too warm down here to wear it, Jim. I want young people to use it to understand the war."

Part One

Sophisticated and deadly, German Navy U-boats cruised the depths of the Atlantic as World War II began. Their powerful torpedoes were the curse of the seas, destroying commercial, civilian and military ships and even threatening American shores.

To maintain the subs and equip them with lethal force, the Nazis placed supply and repair systems throughout Germany and their captured territories. The harbor at Lorient, France, housed one of several vast naval bases along Europe's Atlantic coast, built with layer upon layer of reinforced concrete that surrounded and protected the U-boats and maintenance facilities and resisted all attempts to penetrate it

The Allies knew these submarines had to be stopped.

American workers were on the job 24 hours a day across the United States, scrambling to design and build B-17 bombers and bigger and more effective bunker-buster bombs to destroy the German submarine pens. Fledgling U.S. Army Air Forces crews then flew the aircraft from sites across the United States, northeast to Newfoundland, east to Greenland and finally across the Atlantic to England.

The Army Air Forces were spread throughout England, housed at temporary RAF bases tucked next to formerly peaceful farm fields and villages. Like the planes they serviced, the military installations were built for war, not comfort, featuring hastily-built runways, hangars and barracks.

Enlisting Jan. 5, 1942, a month after the attacks on Pearl Harbor, James "Bud" Wilschke left his home in Chicago, Illinois and won his wings as a bombardier after training in Pocatello, Idaho and Victorville, California. After further instruction in Casper, Wyoming he was assigned to the 305th Bombardment Group of the 8th Air Force and sent to Chelveston, a base about 70 miles north of London.

Bud was an easy-going salt-of-the-earth guy who loved family, sports, and his girl Rosemary. Other than on Scout or family camping trips to Wisconsin and Michigan, he had never been beyond the Chicago area. But there was a war on and young men were called to serve in faraway places.

Bud's younger brother, Bill, 20, enlisted in the U.S. Navy and was stationed at locations in the Pacific theater, where he worked behind the lines to supply food and equipment to troops flying raids over China. Meanwhile, Bill's friend and Rosemary Crandell's brother, George Crandell, 24, served as a young officer aboard the destroyer USS Dale, moored at Ulithi, a small atoll in the South Pacific.

Bud had always been well-liked and enjoyed the camaraderie at the training camps he had just left, so he was puzzled at first by the coolness and distance he felt from the men who were already in place when he arrived overseas. If the mood at Chelveston was somber, it was because by the time Bud joined the war effort, losses of American flyers and planes were already staggering. Day after day, flyers went out on missions and didn't make it back. Nazi anti-aircraft guns were deadly and German fighter planes were becoming expert at shooting down the lumbering B-17 Flying Fortresses. One in four of his peers didn't survive until the end of his tour, by now 25 missions. Bud soon felt the impact of losing buddies that he had breakfast with just that morning.

For Bud, it was the beginning of a great and terrifying wartime odyssey.

Chapter 1

May 17, 1943

Our ship had no fancy name because we were superstitious about fancy names. We figured the big baby without a fancy title like Pistol Packin' Mama or Kitty from Kansas City would fight just as well. Guess you can't tell about those things. —Staff Sergeant Bob Neil

Second Lieutenant Bud Wilschke, a fresh-faced 23-year-old bombardier heading out on his fourth bombing raid, sat in the cramped Plexiglas nose cone of B-17F Flying Fortress #42-5219, surveying the landscape and watching for the enemy. As always on the days they flew missions, he was wakened long before dawn. Still, Bud had displayed the good humor he was known for, encouraging the crew even when he felt like he really needed a lot more sleep. He knew good morale was everybody's business. The air crews were brothers-in-arms whether they had come from the streets of Chicago or a farm in Kansas. When lousy food, unfamiliar surroundings,

James Wilschke in training.

strange accents, encounters with injury and death, or potential loss of a special girl back home all took a toll, *esprit de corps* made the mission possible. Not wanting to let their buddies down, even when they were wounded and terrified, the men fought on bravely as they knew their mates would. When everyone felt their hearts pounding hard, Bud knew they were also seamlessly united in their focus.

"Feathering engine number four."

Although he was in the pilot seat for the first time, Second Lieutenant Harry Indiere, 26, spoke calmly, notifying the rest of the ten-man crew of the very bad news that they were down an engine. The prop on engine four had been racing and the engine had to be shut down.

Bud glanced to his right and could see the propeller blades on the far engine slowly rotate to face edge-first, cutting the drag on the plane. Even with all four 1200 horsepower supercharged radial engines operating perfectly, the big bombers were like plow horses, pulling hard to do their heavy lifting. They could never keep pace with the rest of the formation now. Down to three engines, they were going to need every ounce of power and fuel available just to get them back safely to their base.

Despite their handicapped condition, Indiere and crew continued on the flight plan over St. Malo and the islands of Guernsey and Jersey, southeast across France to Pont Aven, then south-southwest to the target, the French coastal city of Lorient and the U-boat headquarters there. Lorient was already in ruins, bombed three times in 1940 by the RAF, five times in 1942, and 14 times already in 1943, without destroying the sub base.

Bud wore gloves and his heavy flight jacket to help survive the -65F cold in the unpressurized and unheated plane. The leather was stiff at those temperatures but Bud loved the way the jacket kept him warm and cushioned from the sharp angles in the plane. To allow more freedom of movement, flyers usually wore a harness over the jacket and left their parachutes near at hand, expecting to snap them on quickly in the all-too-likely event they had to bail out. Bud had been careful to snap the harness on before he pulled himself into the plane that early morning.

Earlier, at Chelveston, Bud had been up at 4 a.m. for mission-day breakfast and briefing. Not surprisingly, he found himself assigned to a new crew. In his three missions, he had not flown with Indiere, co-pilot Second Lieutenant Joe Boyle, nor with most of the other crew on board that day.

Their "Fort" was assigned the unlucky "Tail-end Charlie" position. Last in the formation even before losing engine four, they were the first pick of the German fighters. Three more squadrons of "Heavies" were ahead of them, 159 B-17s, all focused on reaching

Lorient, 370 miles to the south. It was a dangerous position to be in as they approached the coast of France, dense with anti-aircraft guns and patrolled by German fighter planes with well-trained pilots eager to become "aces." Bud guessed that given such a serious problem with their plane so early in the mission, they would soon abort and return to their airbase at Chelveston.

Looking up from his vantage point in the nose of the plane, Bud could see that their Fort had fallen behind and dropped about 1,000 feet below the group, but Indiere still showed no signs of turning back. They were now outside of the protection of the bomber formation and easier pickings for a fighter attack. He knew this was Indiere's first time in the pilot seat and silently cursed him for taking chances with the crew. *Why the heck are we still trying to complete the mission? We're sitting ducks! Let's live to fight another day!*

Another report came over the intercom: the droll voice of tail-gunner Henry Mitchell.

"Bogeys, no, bandits, 3 o'clock high."

Then, more urgently from waist gunner Dennis Cullinan, "Bogeys, 9 o'clock high."

Cullinan was seeing a squadron of German Focke-Wulf 190 fighter planes quickly closing in from the left, but Mitchell had seen another group of 190s boring in from the right. The FW-190s, fastest fighters of the time, could fire 900 rounds per minute from machine guns and another 450 rounds from the even more deadly cannons, shooting explosive rounds that could burst a plane apart.

The first machine gun rounds strafed through the Fortress. The enemy fighters banked away and backed off briefly while flak from anti-aircraft guns below shook the B-17, shock waves flexing the seams of the great wingspan until it seemed certain to rip apart.

White vapor trails streamed behind as the bombers dropped to the correct altitude for the final run at the drop zone over Lorient, German anti-aircraft shells bursting all around them. From a distance, the flak looked like harmless puffs of dandelion seed but as the bursts got closer, pink and orange explosions hurtled shards of white-hot metal through the fuselage.

"Hang on boys, we're going in!" At last, Indiere steered their ship from the "specified index point" where the bombers turned toward the target without any further evasive action, and handed control of the plane over to Bud. The bombardier's job was to finish guiding the loaded bomber into the target zone and drop the bombs precisely over the target.

Bud touched the jacket pocket where he kept his picture of Rosemary, then left all other concerns behind and focused only on his critical job. Using his new top-secret Norden bombsight to carefully gauge aircraft speed, wind, and altitude, Bud calculated the exact moment he should release the bombs to strike the Nazi sub base. He barely blinked, pacing his breath, steady as a marksman. Time seemed to slow. He focused like never before in his life to get it just right, ignoring the jolts and heaves of the plane as the flak burst around them. While he concentrated, the gunners blasted away at the Focke-Wulfs.

Time to lay the eggs from Uncle Sam.

Bud triggered the release.

"Bombs away!"

He dropped the 5000-pound payload just as more enemy fighters swooped in and ripped the aircraft with repeated bursts of machine gun and cannon fire. As its payload dropped away, the bomber bounced upward. It was time to hustle the wounded plane back to safety in Chelveston and get everything ready for the next mission.

These planes were built to take a terrible beating, coming back to base with shredded tails and wings, nose cones blown away, ripped full of holes until the metal looked like jagged green lace, but still flying. But this time, the enemy fighters quickly caught up and refocused their attack. Cannon shells tore through the plane, destroying the radio operator's station. Tracer bullets streamed past the plane but too many rounds were making hits.

Indiere and Boyle fought to control their Fort while the crew fired furiously at the German attackers with the thirteen .50 caliber machine guns even as more bullets ripped through their own fuselage, leaving daylight shining through. *Get us home now, Harry!*

With bombs away, Bud grabbed his own twin machine guns, took aim and shot back at the swarming FW-190s as flak burst all around. No time to think—his training took over though his heart felt like it would pound its way out of his chest. Machine gun shell casings flew through the air and covered the floor. The air in the plane was hot and thick with choking smoke.

The Fort jumped and shuddered as more flak bursts sent shrapnel slicing through the plane. Fragments bounced off the armor plate of the pilots' chairs and whizzed across the cabin. Numbing cold wind blew through the jagged gaps in the plane as the crew fought on for their lives.

The fatal blows came in a flash. Enemy rounds tore through the control system lines, hydraulic fluids gushed from shredded hoses and caught fire, and the cramped inside of the plane was suddenly ablaze. Oxygen lines ripped open and, like a welding torch, the flames instantly were hot enough to melt the plane itself. The airmen now had only seconds before they would pass out from lack of oxygen. Their extinguishers were useless for the blazes. Control systems now destroyed, the pilots struggled to keep the plane out of a spin, which would pin the flyers helpless against the fuselage until it crashed to earth.

The remaining engines were billowing smoke; the intercom was dead; the noise was deafening. Gunning for the enemy fighters, Bud couldn't tell what was happening to the crew in the rest of the plane. Thick smoke and fumes poured into the nose cone as the bailout bell shrieked. Choking and fighting for breath, the crew struggled to not get burned. Bud already knew what to do. *Out of the plane, now, Bud!* He grabbed his chute and snapped it on the harness around his bomber jacket, crouched down to the escape hatch behind him and underneath the cockpit and kicked it open, exposing the rushing sea far below.

This was Bud's first jump. Practice parachute jumps during training back in the States were too dangerous and airmen too precious. He peered through the hatch at the shimmering blue waters of the Bay of Biscay and could make out the French coast in the distance.

Roy Richards, flight navigator and Bud's friend from training, squeezed past and motioned that he was going up into the nose to get something. Over the roar of the engines, howling wind, searing bullets, constant explosions, the raging fire and deadly fumes, Bud didn't know what Roy said but he couldn't wait to find out. At 27,000 feet, with the air temperature about -35F, it was time to hit the silk. His heart pounding, Bud jumped down through the open hatch as if he had just leaped from a diving board at home in Illinois. With his jacket and chute on, the hatch was just big enough to let him drop through. He slammed into the turbulent slipstream rushing below and instantly was swept behind the doomed plane.

The flaming, smoking bomber flew on for a short while, shedding parts as it sank toward Earth. German fighters continued their chase, firing constantly to make sure of their kill.

Finally, the Fort exploded, tail blowing away from its fuselage. Chunks of aircraft fell, fiery fragments of a man-made meteor. Despite being hammered by the piercing air around him, Bud's heart ached for the crew members who might not escape the doomed plane.

Hurtling towards the water at about 125 miles an hour, Bud gasped for breath in the thin air and fought to keep his wits about him as he positioned to properly free-fall. He had to drop down fast to where he could get more oxygen. He knew to not open the chute too quickly or it would be hit by the plane or tangle the chute. Dropping straight down also foiled any German flyers on the hunt for Allied airmen escaping a damaged plane and made a shorter time for Germans on the ground to race to capture them. *Don't pull the ripcord too soon, Bud! One thousand, two thousand, three thousand . . .*

There was the earth rushing closer. He fought to clear his head.

After an eternity of plummeting and at what seemed the last possible moment, Bud grabbed the big metal D-ring on his chest and gave it a firm yank. The violent jolt from the chute hit him like a hard fist.

Whoosh!

A fabric cloud unfurled and the wind scooped him up, a fragile kite to save his life.

305TH Bomb Group "Can Do"

B17 * 42-5219
FLYING FORTRESS

1. Bombardier James "Bud" Wilschke (Evader)
2. Navigator Roy Richards (KIA)
3. Co-Pilot Joseph B. Boyle (POW)
4. Pilot Harry W. Indiere (POW)
5. Engineer John W. McFarland (KIA)
6. Radio Operator Robert "Bob" Nell (Evader)
7. Ball Turret Gun Walter R. Schenk (KIA)
8. Right Waist Gun Dennis T. Cullinan (KIA)
9. Left Waist Gun John D. Norris (KIA)
10. Tail Henry A. Mitchell, Jr. (KIA)

Bud had bailed out over open water. Descending under his chute to the level of nearby birds, air currents pushed him northeast over the coast.

In the distance, dogfights raged on and he could see other smoking, crippled planes and parachutes dropping from them. His ears rang from the explosions as he glided on the wind and pulled on the shroud lines as hard as he could to steer toward the coast. Lower, over land and coming down fast, he tried to maneuver to an open field. Instead he headed like a missile for a stone farmhouse and barn directly in his path. As he strained for any control, the ground came rushing up, until—BANG! —he crash-landed into a wooden split rail fence. Bud's world went black.

Below the dogfight, French farmers and villagers watched the battles in the sky. On the ground below, young Jean Gauter, child of a multi-generational family of farmers in Kerbellec, Brittany, was being cared for in his family's home while his 25-year-old mother was tending the cows in the family's rapeseed field. The Germans had set up a military camp on the southeastern border of the Gauter farm, to provide easy access to the Paris-Quimper railway line. Because of this unfortunate proximity to the enemy, the Gauters always kept an eye out for any ominous events around them. The stress of the family's involuntary co-existence with the Germans was believed to have contributed to the debilitating stroke Jean's grandfather had recently suffered.

Late that morning, May 17, 1943, Jean's mother suddenly heard the warning siren from the German station known as Pipark, less than a kilometer away. Not knowing what the danger was or from where it was coming, she ran for refuge in the adjacent patch of woods and crouched low behind a stump.

Above her, air combat suddenly raged between an American bomber and German fighters. The roar of engines and scream of the plane spinning out of control were peppered by the drumbeat of machine guns and cannon fire. Bullets and flak fragments rained down like hail, splashing up the plowed soil around her.

Jean's mother saw the plane disintegrate in mid-air just after several parachutes escaped.

Later, a German soldier hunting for any possible survivors spotted her as she returned to her herd of cows and rushed over to question her at gunpoint. Mme. Gauter coolly replied: "I saw nothing at all; I did not want to see anyway!"

In fact, she had seen an American airman fall in the very field where her cows placidly grazed. The man fell hard into the plowed earth of her rapeseed field, his chute collapsed and useless. Mme. Gauter's neighbors later marveled at the impression his body left in the dirt, one man testing it and remarking that his body fit exactly into the flyer's outline. A second flyer fell a short distance away in a wooded area across railroad tracks from where she farmed, his chute snagged in a tree. A third airman was found a few days later in a trench nearby, shot in the head. Another observer described watching his body, on fire, fluttering as it fell to the ground. The tail section of the big plane fell nearby. Another man's body was found in the wreckage. The bomber's body and engines fell further on with more crew inside.

Gauter and his brother, Joseph, gathered up some of the more manageable pieces of the plane's debris, scattered over the embankments.

After the smoke cleared, there were four survivors: the pilot, Harry Indiere; copilot, Joseph Boyle, radio man; Robert Neil and James Wilschke, "Bud."

German soldiers saw Boyle land near them and captured him immediately. He spent the night in jail in Auray, near where the plane crashed. The next day he was transferred to another town, Vannes, and reunited with Indiere, whose right leg was injured after his tangled chute was cut from the tree where it had been caught. After interrogation, both were sent to a POW camp, Stalag Luft 3.

Bob Neill and Bud evaded capture and were considered by the military to be "Missing in Action" (MIA). After six months, they would be considered dead.

Chapter 2

First Helpers

ACHTUNG!
All males who come to the aid, either directly or indirectly, of the
crews of enemy aircraft coming down in parachutes, or having made
a forced landing, helps in their escape, hides them, or comes to their
aid in any fashion, will be shot on the spot.
Women who render the same help will be sent to
concentration camps in Germany.
—Notice posted in France in 1941

Bud parachuted into the Brittany peninsula on the northwestern edge of France, a picturesque region of small farming villages scattered over gently rolling landscape. The Bretons, a proud, ancient Celtic culture with their own language still in use to this day, deeply hated the Nazis and their forced occupation, now in its third year. Because it was a prosperous farm region, food was more plentiful in Brittany than in the larger cities where it was rationed and increasingly scarce.

Bud landed with an evasion kit specifically designed to help downed flyers. His kit contained malt tablets, bouillon powder, chocolate, Benzedrine tablets for fatigue, matches, adhesive tape, chewing gum, a water bottle with purification tablets, a hacksaw file, a small red purse with 2,000 French francs, two passport-sized photos of him in civilian clothes to build identity documents, a compass disguised as a shirt button, silk maps that were waterproof, durable and quiet when opened, and silk kerchiefs with the American flag and a printed message in multiple languages: "I am an American and do not speak your language. I need food, shelter and assistance. I will not harm you. I bear no malice toward your people. If you will help me, my government will reward you."

Bud and his fellow airmen had been briefed before their flights and instructed on what to do if they found themselves in enemy territory—move away from the crash site as soon as possible, and trust no one. If at all possible, avoid Resistance groups and take your chances with individuals or single families.

Whenever a flyer was repatriated, he was carefully interviewed to find out who had helped him and how to make escape and evasion more successful for the soldiers who came after. Records of these debriefing interviews later assisted the American government in compensating French helpers for their courageous efforts.

"Américain ou allemand?! Américain ou allemand?!"

American or German? As Bud came to, a grizzled, middle-aged man wearing overalls and a tweed cap stood about twenty feet away, pointing an ancient-looking double-barreled shotgun at him. His parachute had been taken off and moved away from him, probably by the same farmer.

"Mister, I'm an American."

Bud held his hands as high as he could.

"I don't speak French."

The man spoke in English.

"What are you doing here?"

"I am an American airman." Bud pantomimed floating to the ground as if the man with the shotgun did not understand. He was new at this game. "My plane was shot down over the bay and I parachuted here."

The farmer's face softened. "Must go. No good here. You must go."

He lowered his gun and motioned Bud to follow. Bud slowly struggled to his feet, his heart pounding, ears ringing and leg throbbing from his crash onto the fence. Still in shock, he limped after the farmer. With every searing step, he wondered if his leg were broken.

He agreed with the farmer. It was no good being in the open where German patrols were sure to be looking for survivors. Bud wasn't sure if any others of his crew had bailed out in time.

Struggling to keep up with the farmer, he stumbled painfully through the uneven field toward a stone house with a few small farm buildings, oblivious to the picturesque soft green rolling hills and carefully-tended fields that extended to the sea a mile or so to the south.

"My name is James Wilschke. Bud Wilschke."

"I am Mathurin Diabat," said the man, hurrying Bud through the grass, never slowing his urgent pace toward the farm.

"I help you American. I hate *les boches*. They kill our good men, take our women and children away. You can fight them again."

"Listen, Mr. Diabat, I hurt my leg pretty bad. Don't know if I can go much further."

"It is not far now. We must hide you."

They reached a small barn not far from the main house. Inside the weathered door, Bud saw pieces of lumber and assorted horse tack. Diabat pointed to the sizeable horse cart in a corner of the back of the barn.

"You stay there. No noise."

Diabat helped Bud into the cart and covered him with sweet smelling clover hay. It was a relief for Bud to take the weight off his leg.

"Back soon," the farmer said. Diabat pulled the barn door closed behind him and Bud was alone in darkness. Slowly, he caught his breath, but his senses were alert, his heart still pounding.

The morning had been sunny and pleasant on the Diabat farm until the war flashed across the sky. Now Diabat found himself facing grave danger as he tried to help the wounded American. He hurried toward the small village less than a mile away, along small goat tracks through the woods. It did not appear that soldiers were headed to his farm. They seemed to be rushing toward the pillar of smoke where a large plane had crashed. He had briefly seen a couple of other parachutes disappear closer to the village, moments before he had seen Bud slam into the fence line on his land.

Diabat did what he could to help the Allies fight the Nazi invaders. Two months earlier, his brother-in-law and a family from the north were publicly executed and his sister and niece were dragged away, never to be seen again. The Germans had suspected that his sister's family had given food to another family escaping their own village after it was burned to the ground. The cruel retribution inflamed Diabat's desire to resist.

Public notices declared that any French man found to be helping the allies would be shot on the spot and women would be
deported to concentration camps. To encourage betrayal of neighbors, rewards of 10,000 francs or more were promised. The fleeing
Diabat family had been discovered when someone in the village
reported them. Similarly, many Resistance groups had been infiltrated and broken up as neighbor turned on neighbor until members were dead, deported or fleeing for their lives.

By helping this American, Diabat was risking not only his life
but the lives of his family and the people in the village.

As two figures approached, Diabat quickly jumped behind a
hedgerow.

Soldiers looking for the American? The two figures were almost
upon him. He listened intently.

"You think you saw the man fall from the plane this way?"

It was the voice of Pierre Sauvet. Diabat startled the men as he
jumped out of his hiding place.

"Pierre, it is me, Mathurin."

"*Mon Dieu*, you gave us a scare."

The other man was Michel Bertrand. Both were teachers in the
village. They too were rebels against the Nazis. But like Diabat, they
were careful to keep their ideas and activities quiet.

"Patrols are everywhere," Sauvet warned. "We saw the planes
fighting and the American one come crashing down. It looked like
some of the debris and maybe one of the airmen landed on your
farm. Then the plane sank over Ploemel and toward Brec'h."

"Indeed. The American survived but he may have a broken leg.
He is hidden in a cart back at my barn."

"He cannot stay there, Mathurin. There is a patrol not far behind
us. They will hunt until they have found all of them, dead or alive,"
Bertrand urged. "We must get him out of there."

The three quickly made their way to the shed where Diabat
looked around carefully before pulling the door open just far
enough to enter. Inside, Bud remained in Diabat's cart, still under
the clover. Diabat called to him and Bud brushed the clover away.

"We must find a safer place," Sauvet said. "They will find him
there for sure."

He turned to Bud. "What is your name?"

Sauvet was proud of his English, but this was his first time talking to an American.

"My name is Lieutenant James Wilschke. They call me 'Bud.' He pulled his ID from his jacket pocket. Sauvet examined it and handed the card back to Bud.

"I saw others like you land near the tracks on the other side of our village. There was a train passing through. The *boche* grabbed two men and took them to the train."

"Could you get a good look at them?"

"No, it is too far from my window in town. But the men seemed able to walk."

It was a relief to know that some of his crew were alive. They would most likely become prisoners of war but at least they had a lifeline of hope, one more chance to stay alive until the next day, and the next, and the next. Bud nodded to Sauvet with gratitude.

"We will keep our ears open," promised Bertrand. Turning to Diabat, he added "If we hear they suspect the American is at your farm, we will send word. He needs to find a safer place and figure out how to get back to his base."

"What shall I do with him in the meantime?" Diabat asked.

As they spoke, two Germans on motorcycles passed nearby. There was no time to waste.

"We have to return to the school or we will be missed. He has an injured leg and we will see if someone can look at it. But just now it does not seem to be a severe injury since he can place a little weight on it."

At first, they helped Bud limp toward a field of rye, but realized the Germans would see trails of their movement through the tall grass and weeds. They backed out and quickly moved him to the corner of a tall, dense, hawthorn hedgerow covered with thick ferns. The sharp thorns made it difficult to move among the branches, but the men pulled a space open and Bud eased his way in, his leg throbbing. His thick flight jacket and pants helped protect him against the thorns. He pulled his collar up to protect his face and neck.

"Wait until I return," Diabat said. Sauvet and Bertrand set off for their school.

Diabat went back to his home and asked his wife, Séraphine, to put on a pot of tea.

"Did you find anything, husband? Were there survivors?"

Séraphine moved quickly around her simple kitchen, watching her husband, preparing his meal.

"I found an injured American named James. I hid him until I can figure out what to do."

A teacup shattered on the floor.

"You brought him here? If they find him, they will take us away for sure, or worse." She reached for a broom. "You know what happened to my brother! How could you be so foolish?"

"It is the right thing to do."

Diabat himself cleaned up the mess on the floor.

"We have discussed this. We are farmers and we cannot hope to win this war ourselves. If the *boche* win, who knows what will become of us? The best thing we can do for now is to help those that will fight for us."

"But what about André and Léontine and Alice? Do you want to see them taken away to some camp?"

"Of course not. I am being careful. Pierre and Michel are helping me. We will move the American as soon as it is safe."

André, the couple's son, came rushing into the house, dragging his youngest sister behind him and slamming the door shut. He was panting loudly and Alice was trembling, her eyes wide with fear as she clutched her doll.

"They are here Papa."

There was a loud banging. Before Diabat could answer, the door burst open with a crash. He recognized the four soldiers who had previously taken his family members away and their Nazi officer. They stormed into the small kitchen and glared at the family. There was barely room for everyone. Their faces were close to Diabat's, their odor invading his senses.

"An airman landed in your field. We could not find him, but saw his parachute come down here. Where have you hidden him? Don't be a fool. If you give him up immediately, we might be able to over-look your violation with some minor consequences. We will search everywhere. If you do not give him up and we find him, I will shoot you immediately. Do you understand?"

Diabat knew that even if he turned in the American, he would be shot or hanged as a reminder of what happened to dissidents.

"I don't know what you are talking about. We heard the planes fighting and ran in here to take cover. We are not so foolish as to get in the way of such things. I have seen no one."

A brief moment of silence and the officer sneered, pulled out his Luger pistol and grabbed young Alice by the hair.

"Where have you hidden him? If we find that you have hidden or helped him, you will all meet your Maker, farmer. We shall see."

The officer snapped out commands and two soldiers began tearing the farmhouse apart. The other two went outside to search the barn and farm. The officer held Alice's hair for several minutes while the search continued, then pushed her away suddenly. Alice only whimpered softly. Séraphine, who had been huddled in the corner, comforting the children, drew Alice into her arms where the girl sobbed softly, while André looked ready to jump at anyone if they came close to his kin.

While the officer held the Diabat family hostage, his soldiers climbed apple trees around the property, searching for any evidence of a downed airman. As Bertrand and Sauvet had feared, the soldiers thrust their bayonets into the cart of clover. Somehow, they found nothing. Finally, one of the men returned to the kitchen and whispered in the officer's ear. His face twisted in disgust.

"I suppose this is your lucky day, farmer. If you see any Americans or hear of any being hidden by your neighbors, you are to report it to me immediately. We will reward you for your loyalty. On the other hand, let me remind you, if we find out that you have lied or kept secrets from us, we will burn your farm to the ground with you tied to it."

Diabat watched the men straddle their motorcycles and head back to the village. He and his family quietly put their house back in order. He knew the Nazis could be watching his house, lying in wait for him to make a move and expose his secret. Diabat patiently measured the moments until it was completely dark. He knew the farm well enough to traverse it without a light.

"Come André, I need your help. Séraphine, please get some food and blankets together. I am going to move him to the loft."

Séraphine only nodded.

Bud had not moved from his spot for hours. He had heard the enemy searching the farm as he lay in the thicket, watched insects, smelled the farm and worried about his throbbing leg. He thought about Rosemary and his family and his fellow airmen. He listened to movements in the fields and at the farm nearby, though his ears still rang from the destruction of his plane. He dared not move a muscle though his leg hurt and his bruised body ached for food and water. Now it was dark and getting colder. He heard the German motorcycles leave the farm. The night went quiet again. He kept listening. Then he was startled to hear his name by a voice that seemed right next to his ear.

"American?" whispered Diabat. "Bud?"

"Yes, I am here."

"Can you walk?"

"I think so, with some help."

Diabat and André helped Bud crawl out of the thicket and limp through the darkness. He slowly and painfully pulled his way up a wooden ladder into the loft of the barn. Séraphine told Alice to bring a few of her papa's clothes to Bud's new hideaway along with bean soup and bread. Diabat and André made a bed of hay and blankets.

"When I leave, pull up the ladder and sleep. No candle, no matches."

In the quiet, fragrant darkness, Bud zipped his jacket, turned his collar up, pulled the blankets over him, and settled into the hay. He prayed fervently that he would make it back home and see Rosemary once more. Exhausted, he slept.

Chapter 3

Chicago

My grandparents registered their house as a "Tourist Home" for vacationers—vacationing despite the Depression—to stay in, and pay for, while visiting the [1933] World's Fair. Every few weeks a new family would arrive, having signed up at the visitors' center and been shown a list of available tourist homes. No regulations, no inspections, and apparently no warnings or qualms about the chicken-slaughtering going on in the basement. So it would have been normal for my father [Bill Wilschke] and uncle [Bud Wilschke] on any bright summer day to go home to total strangers abruptly placed in the two upstairs bedrooms, as well as at the breakfast table. The boys were sent to sleep in a quickly constructed basement bedroom (again, the basement), while my grandparents moved to the back porch. -- The income from "roomers" proved so helpful that the home stayed open to them for as long as my grandmother, even past widowhood and past Depression, owned the house.
—Nancy Wilschke, Bud's cousin, *Meet Me at the Fair*

James Wilschke 1942.

James Spencer "Bud" Wilschke was 21 years old when the news came that Pearl Harbor had been attacked.

Bud was a rugged youth who loved scouting and camping. He had been a champion high school athlete in track and field, swimming and football. Well-regarded by his teachers, he was regularly entrusted with various jobs and personal errands for the high school staff.

Like most Americans, the Wilschkes had hard times during the Depression years. All the kids had chores; Bud always had jobs. His least favorite was picking up horse manure from the street to spread in his family garden.

In high school, Bud worked summers as a Lake Michigan lifeguard before being hired at Miner-Dunn Hamburgers, a popular Chicago diner. Starting as a short order cook, Bud mastered the technique of making tasty hamburgers, French fries, and milkshakes. He was a hardworking, dependable employee and eventually worked his way up to assistant manager.

Rosemary Crandell, Bud's sweetheart, graduated from Hirsch High School a year after Bud did. The Wilschkes and Crandells lived about a mile apart on

Rosemary Crandell 1942.

Chicago's South Side. Bud and Rosemary met through her brother, George, co-captain of the 1937 Hirsch football team for which Bud played center. Rosemary and her girlfriends watched admiringly and sometimes flirted with the boys at the practices and games.

Rosemary was Bud's dream girl — when he met her a spark went through him that never went away. By all accounts, once they started dating, Bud never looked at another woman again. He was proud that Rosemary was considered one of the best jitterbug dancers at Hirsch High. Their favorite date was to go to the Willowbrook or Trianon Ballrooms where they could dance to the big band sounds of Spike Jones, Jimmy and Tommy Dorsey and Glenn Miller.

When Bud was due to graduate from his Army Air Forces officer training, Rosemary made the trip to California for the ceremony and pinned Wings on his uniform. Rosemary said "yes" when Bud proposed but agreed to wait until after the war to get married. In case he didn't make it home, Bud didn't want Rosemary to be a war widow. Instead of a ring, Bud gave her a delicate bracelet he'd bought and had engraved at the PX. It wasn't a fancy piece of jewelry but it had a small emblem of bombardier's wings on it and their initials, "JSW" to "RRC." Bud hoped it showed how much he loved her.

After high school, Rosemary was employed as a switchboard operator at Sears, Roebuck and Co. In 1943, she worked as a secretary and lived at home with her parents, Harry and Mabel Crandell.

Mabel was an amateur artist and homemaker. Harry had held onto his management job with the Illinois Bell Telephone Co. throughout the Depression.

Rosemary's brother George enlisted in Navy ROTC while he studied at the University of Chicago. He was assigned to the USS Dale, a destroyer based in the northern Pacific patrolling from the coastline and islands off Alaska, to the South Pacific islands.

Bright and eager to learn and achieve, Rosemary had hoped to attend college after graduating from high school. However, her father believed that sending girls to university was a waste of money and refused to support her ambitions. Instead, she completed a two-year program at Woodrow Wilson Business College. She was hired at a Chicago realty office and lived in her parents' home, waiting for Bud to return.

Rosemary celebrates with Bud.

A talented seamstress, Rosemary also passed time making almost all her own outfits. The Crandells were avid dog lovers and Terry, their lively Affenpinscher terrier, helped keep Rosemary's spirits up.

While Rosemary waited for news from her fiancé, Bud's regular crew pilot, Captain Allan Walker, sat in his barracks and thought about the events of the day. He had returned safely from the Lorient mission to Chelveston, the English air base that Bud's plane had flown out of. Walker had been piloting a different B-17 in the formation and lived through the German fighter attack on the squadron. He knew he had lost friends and fellow flyers that day but didn't know what had happened to all of them.

Like Bud, Walker was a sober and responsible man. He cared about his crew, even those who hadn't flown with him that day. He thought about Bud's plane breaking up and parachutes dropping away from it and decided to send a letter to Rosemary.

Rosemary and Terry, her Affenpinscher.

364 Bomb Sq.
305 Bomb Esp.
634 A.P.O.
May 17th, 1943

Dear Rosemary,
This is a hard letter for me to write and I know just as hard for you to receive.

Today Richards and Jim [Bud Wilschke] went on a raid and had motor trouble right over the target and all ten members of the crew were forced to bail out, which they all did successfully.

I know all ten parachutes opened which means all the crew got down to the ground alright.

They have a chance of escaping to a neutral country or else becoming prisoners of war, just depending on the situation on the ground where they landed.

One point in our favor is that once a person goes through what Jim will and I'm certain that he'll get back to England O.K., that he will not have to fight in that theater of war again and he goes back to the states.

If there is anything that I can do for you please let me know.
Sincerely yours,
Allan P Walker
Jim's Pilot

Reflecting on the letter, Rosemary realized that her job from then on was to hold a positive frame of mind and do her best to will Bud back home safely. The dread of every waiting family was a knock on the door from a somber chaplain or uniformed official delivering a death notification. Even considering it for a moment brought grief and tears.

"Mom, I don't know what to hold on to," she shared with her mother over a cup of morning coffee. "The waiting, day in and day out, to hear some news, any news — it seems endless."

"I know Dear, we don't know how soon Bud will return or when the war will end, but we know that our soldiers are fighting the good fight and have to stand up to an evil enemy. Our part is to hope, pray, contribute to the war effort and try not to worry, hard as that may seem in the moment."

Rosemary recognized that Walker's kind letter was meant to buoy her spirits and extend a glimmer of hope. With gratitude for this token of optimism, she vowed to keep that flame of hope burning steadily. She would be resolute in her devotion, and like the "Rosie the Riveters" on the home front, do her modest part in contributing to a successful outcome for the Allied troops in the worldwide theater of war.

Bud's mother, Mabel Wilschke, had received the official cablegram and shared the heartbreaking news with Rosemary. Bud was listed as Missing in Action. His name and photo were published in the Chicago Tribune along with other MIAs. Beyond six months, Bud would be presumed killed in action. Not knowing and the "What If'" wondering weighed on Rosemary the most.

Rosemary instinctively touched and held the bracelet on her right arm. She recalled how Bud had given it to her only months ago. She lit a candle and placed it in the front room window. She imagined Bud walking through the door and conclusively blowing it out.

Chapter 4

Joining Bob Neil

*I was part of a pick-up crew of relative strangers and following the
briefing that morning, we loaded up the airplane . . . it was still
before dawn . . . we were flying with Harry Indiere, and in the
tail we had Sgt. Mitchell . . . those two were the only ones I had
seen before . . . it was truly a pick-up crew.*
—Second Lieutenant Joe Boyle, War Eagles

The next morning, when Diabat returned to the loft, he had good
news.

"I heard in the village there was another man found and hidden
like you."

As he sat up too quickly, a sharp pain from his injured leg
gripped Bud.

"Who was it? What was his name? What did he look like?"

Diabat shook his head.

"I do not know anything about the man other than he is safe for
now. I hid your parachute."

He handed Bud tattered overalls, a plaid shirt and a vest. "You
wear these and I will hide your clothes."

Bud was reluctant to give up his flying clothes. It meant giving
up the gear that had been designed to protect him, and being caught
out of uniform could mean execution as a spy.

At the same time, wearing his uniform made him impossible
to hide. And his heavy leather shearling-lined jacket, like a suit of
armor in the wrong place, would not help him much down on the
ground. He felt a loss when he took it off, removed his escape and
evasion kit and picture of Rosemary, and tucked them into the shirt
Diabat provided. He gave the jacket to Diabat, along with his gloves
and uniform. He pulled on an old pair of Diabat's work shoes.

"Please eat and get dressed. It is not safe for my family to keep
you here."

The morning dragged on. Bud knew this stranger was risking his life and his family's lives by helping him. Rain began to fall. He did not want to cause Diabat any harm, but Bud needed to make his way back to England. For the moment, the combined smells of fresh air and earthy farm were somehow comforting.

Around midday, Diabat returned.

"How is your leg?"

"Not sure it's not broken, but I can put some weight on it. I don't think I could run though. And my ribs really hurt."

"Some trusted friends will take you where it is safe. You will need to get back into the cart."

Diabat supported Bud as he hopped along on his hobbled leg.

"I cannot thank you enough for what you have done for me, Mister. I hope someday I can return the favor."

Diabat began covering him with hay.

"You owe me nothing, just help us be free. That will be thanks enough."

Diabat guided the horse-drawn cart down a dirt lane seldom traveled by patrols, slowly making their way along the rutted path, under a canopy of trees growing up from both sides. The afternoon sun burned brightly, but it was more than heat drenching his shirt with sweat, it was fear. The German patrols were looking for the men and might look harder than they typically did and go deeper into the farm country he and the American, Bud, were traveling.

Diabat's cart approached an unmarked crossroad in the woods. One way went toward town and the other toward some neighboring farms. Diabat looked down the lane and saw what he was looking for, a well-used sedan parked near the road toward the village, hidden in the tall boxwood trees.

"They are here, come with me."

Diabat helped Bud from the cart. As they approached the automobile, Bud wondered if this man could be turning him in to save his family. Or even for a reward? That seemed far-fetched, since he could have brought the Nazis right to him in the barn. There had been a patrol yesterday and he had kept Bud's presence a secret, but how much was this stranger willing to risk? Bud knew he really had no control at that moment.

The driver waved Diabat off, so the farmer stopped walking toward the car and instead turned back to his cart. *I hope I made the right choice about this American. I have done my part and the rest is up to you, dear God.*

It was Bud's turn to sweat as he saw Diabat turn back, climb on his cart and cluck to his horse as he turned back home. Was this it? If the car were full of Germans, he prayed they would take him away rather than shoot him on the spot. He was not so much afraid of death, but he really wanted to see his gal Rosemary again.

Bud was not prepared for what happened next. The rear car door opened, revealing a man peeking out from under a pile of blankets. With the sun in Bud's eyes, it was impossible for him to see who it was.

"Come on Bud! Jerries are everywhere! Get inside, we need to move!"

Bud didn't realize he had been holding his breath until it burst from him with a sob of relief. He was never so glad to see anyone in his life! He crawled into the car, wincing as he drew his leg inside and under the blankets. Next to him on the floor sat Staff Sergeant Robert Neil, 21, the radioman from the plane.

Bud choked back his tears and hugged Bob, but words could not find their way from his throat.

"It's okay buddy," his fellow crew member assured him. "We're going to get out of this mess, or die trying."

As their driver pulled back onto the road, for the first time since the plane crashed, Bud felt real hope. From what he knew, Bob was sharp, and would be a terrific partner. Maybe they would get out of France after all.

As they drove quickly down the wooded road, Bud took a better look at Bob. Like a lot of guys fresh from the States, Bob had grown

Robert Neil 1943.

a mustache like the fashionable RAF crewmen wore. Now, his face and hands were covered with rough bandages, but it was obvious that he had been burned. Bud noticed that Bob no longer had that trademark mustache, and guessed it had burned off in the fire. Bob was grimacing with pain.

"What happened?"

"Oh, do you mean the nice sunburn I got?" Bob tried to laugh. "Trust me, it hurts a lot worse than it looks."

"I don't remember too much of what happened," Bob continued. "Everything seemed to happen so fast. Looks like I tried to put out the fire in the bomb bay with my hands and face. I could see one of the waist gunners, maybe Cullinan, on his back, bleeding badly, his face mask torn off. I don't know what happened next. I woke up flying through thin air and yanked my rip cord and thank God it worked.

"You know in flight school they talk about bailing from a plane and how we should land. But I suppose I wasn't paying close attention. It was an express ride going down with no stops at middle floors.

"The chute finally popped and slowed me down a bit. I remember parts of the old bird flaming past me. One of the Jerry fighters sized me up but must have decided not to kill me. After a few mid-air flips, I landed gracefully face first in some field, dazed, but in one piece. Maybe mud is good for burns, eh?"

"How did you find your way to these guys?"

The two "guys" in the front seat hadn't said a word. Bud supposed they either didn't understand English or maybe they were just listening closely.

"Our bird went on beyond me but it was spinning and sinking fast," Bob said. "I heard it explode and turned to see it break up. On the ground, plane parts were burning everywhere around me and I knew I had to find shelter. A big crowd of French people gathered around. They were excited and happy to see me, but that scared the hell out of me too.

"One old man took my chute and made it disappear. Then I walked down the lane until someone suddenly told me I had to hide in some bushes. A couple of Jerries with rifles went by on bicycles, looking for me somewhere else. I asked for some civilian clothes and one of the men brought me cider and food. People came to see me all day long, like I was an exhibit in a museum.

"About dark, I figured it was time to move. I got a cue the Jerries were coming back looking for me. I saw a little chicken coop not too far away and made my way in there and hid as deep in the straw and manure as I could get. A patrol with dogs was there in minutes, looking around the farm, hunting for me. The people said there were Germans staying everywhere around us. Maybe it was the chicken manure, or maybe it was time for their knockwurst, but they didn't look hard enough.

"After the patrol left, I started walking again. I lay down in a haystack in a field and could hear flak going off above me. Then a bunch of dogs started barking and I figured it was time to keep moving before someone came to check on what they were mad about. I started walking again and M. Bassereau there came out of his house and called out to me."

Bob nodded toward the driver, who gave a small wave, never taking his eyes from the road and surroundings.

The sneaky Frogs were just listening, Bud observed to himself, as Bob resumed his story.

"He took me inside his home and his wife bandaged me up the best she could and got me some clothes to wear. Pierre told me I had to shave my mustache, because French men don't wear them. He scraped that razor right over the top of my toasted hide. Hid me until morning. Said another of my crew had been found and here I am. I tried to keep my boots and flight jacket, but they told me it was too dangerous, so we dug a hole and buried them behind the chicken coop."

"Right. Hated to give up my jacket and gear—but we'd stick out like a sore thumb," agreed Bud. "This way maybe the Jerries won't know who we are. What about the other crew?"

Bob looked away. "They found a couple of bodies, badly burned. Said two other men were picked up by the Jerries and put on a train, but I don't know who they were. They said one of them got his chute caught in a tree. How did you get away?"

As the car rumbled along on the bumpy lane, Bud told the story. "Well, we can assume it's just you and me who are free at the moment, so let's figure out what's the best way home," Bud concluded as they rode as passengers, presumably toward the coast and a place unknown to both of them, entrusting themselves to people they had not met before. They staked their lives on the belief that the French people would do whatever they could to help them and whatever it took to free their country from evil.

Part Two

Chapter 5

Missing in Action

While in hiding, study your maps, locate your position,
and plan your further moves.
Rest until you are entirely composed, have decided where
you are, have estimated the situation, and then
determine what you intend to do next.
—Classified escape and evasion instructions

Their driver, M. François Carlach, headed south to what Bud and Bob learned was Saint-Pierre-Quiberon, a tiny seaside village on a narrow, ten-mile-long peninsula stretching south into the Atlantic.

Bob spoke a few words to Carlach as they arrived at one of the cottages just outside of town. Bud couldn't understand most of it. The men spoke softly in French and finally Bob turned to Bud, "They have to leave us here. They're afraid our presence in their town is too much of a risk."

In the fading light, Carlach got out of the car and quickly walked to the door of a large two-story stucco cottage with brick trim and a red tiled roof.

"He said we can stay here. It's vacant now. A woman and her father, a doctor from the village, are waiting for us inside. He said we need to move on when we have rested and recovered some."

Carlach returned from the home with a middle-aged woman and two brawny boys who lifted Bud from the car and helped him inside, where Bud could see a table, a couple of chairs and a small lantern. Dark curtains covered the windows. A pot on the table held a stew of leeks, potatoes and chicken. The aroma made Bud suddenly realize how hungry he was.

In the dim light, a short man wearing small spectacles and a hat with a single plume gestured to Bob to sit, and began looking at the injuries to his hands and face. Bud sat at the table and was given a bowl of stew. No longer needed, chauffeur Carlach quietly slipped out the back.

Bob winced and bit down on a roll of cloth to handle the pain. The woman and her boys assisted the doctor as best they could, putting fresh dressings on Bob's burns and keeping a silent vigil of support. LeMouroux offered him a small tablet and water and spoke a few words to Bob.

"This is M. Valentine LeMouroux and he wants to help us," Bob told Bud.

LeMouroux said a few words to Bob and then attended to Bud, pushing gently on his leg and feeling his ribs. He patted Bud on the shoulder and offered a few more encouraging words in French, and left quickly with his daughter and grandsons. Bud was confused and made a mental note to ask Bob to teach him some French.

"Well?" asked Bud.

Maybe later. He could see that Bob was falling asleep, probably aided by the medicine.

In a quiet voice, his eyes half-lidded with drowsiness, Bob replied, "He said you and I will both be okay. This is supposed to be a vacant house. We should stay away from the windows and not go outside. We can't build a fire or the neighbors will notice. He will send one of his grandsons, or someone else from the village at least once a day to bring us food and check on us. He will be back in a few days to check my burns . . . "

The last statement tapered off into a light snore. Bud limped over to the window and peered carefully through the curtains. He could not see anything around them, not even any lights from the village, which he estimated was about a mile away.

Bud reached into the pocket of Diabat's old shirt and pulled out the silk map of France he had been hiding in Diabat's shirt. In the dim lantern light, he saw where their current very temporary home of Saint-Pierre-Quiberon was. He could see that England wasn't far away across water as the crow flies but they couldn't possibly get there on their own. Even though he and Bob seemed safe for the moment, the route back to England meant they had to deal with

German patrols on the shore and would need a boat to transport them via the Bay of Biscay to the English Channel.

Over the next three weeks, the flyers, in pain from bruised or broken ribs and injuries everywhere from the series of physical traumas from the dogfight, fire, bailout and landing, slept up to 20 hours a day. Bud's leg began to hurt less when he rested—until he had to walk on it. Bob's burns were especially painful. Thanks to LeMouroux's first aid and pain medicine, he felt he was healing while some of the pain was dulled. Their ears slowly stopped ringing and hearing gradually returned to normal.

Despite their youth, both Bud and Bob were trained, smart, serious and had embraced the attitudes and discipline of military service. They worked at and for the most part succeeded at not complaining. Most difficult was to keep the shock of the catastrophic end of the mission from engulfing them with vivid memories and sensations. Unbidden, again and again, in the daytime and more so in the dark of night, each man saw and heard the rush of events as the plane was destroyed. Their muscles fought to respond to the danger and perform their duty. They relived and grieved the loss of their fellow flyers. They woke from vivid nightmares, hoping they had not been too loud and called attention to their presence as they fought to survive in their harrowing dreams.

Days were filled with conversation, a welcome distraction from recent memories. Unable to even look out the windows much less go outside, the flyers spent hours every day plotting how they would make their way up the coast across Brittany to reach a boat to England. It now seemed the quickest route.

Bud and Bob had not known each other before the Lorient mission, having flown with other crews on other planes. Once in the air, everyone was focused on their job, and even though a flight took many hours there was little time for chatter. After the crash and on the ground together 24-7 in France, they had time to learn about each other and make sense of what had happened to them.

"Where's home for you?" Bud wondered.

"Grew up in Providence, Rhode Island. My mom, little sister, and an older brother and two older sisters still live there. How about you?"

"Chicago, South Side. My mom and two half-sisters still live there. My brother is in the Pacific."

"Where's your dad then?" Bob asked.

Bud sighed and looked away for a moment before he replied.

"Things didn't go so well for my dad. Max Gustav Theodore Wilschke. He was born in Berlin and moved to the States as a young guy. His hard feelings about Germany stayed with him all his life. We had a mean old rooster who strutted around in our chicken flock. My dad named him "Der Kaiser." And boy did he hate Hitler! Dad ran a photography studio until the business dried up, then did all kinds of odd jobs. Sometimes the money was hard to come by, but we never lost our house. I started working as a kid. When times were bad, we ate lard sandwiches and felt really lucky to have that. As time went on, dad had more and more trouble with liquor. Probably had something to do with why he died a couple of years ago."

"Yeah, my dad's gone too."

Bob's sadness had a sharp edge that matched Bud's.

"William Hannah Neil. When I was about nine, he was working in a local garage. I guess he was a great mechanic. He and my mom had already saved up enough to own their own house. Then the fire happened. A light bulb broke while dad was working in the pit under a car. Lots of gas and oil was soaked into the dirt. Went up like a torch. Never woke up. Never had a chance."

Bob's emotion was always near the surface for him. You could hear it in his voice.

"Then the same thing almost happened to me, huh?"

"Mom never let on much about the story. She kind of locked herself up inside after dad died. Wouldn't let us talk about him after that, never would tell us anything about him. Got rid of all the pictures of him and told us to just get busy with growing up and studying. I was lucky one of my sisters hid a picture of him and would let me see it sometimes.

"Mom was pregnant with my baby sister when the fire happened. No time for grief for her or for us. It was just too much for her. Then the Depression hit, and it all just crushed her."

"You lost your dad really young," said Bud. "I was 20 when my dad died, three years ago. Gave me a chance to grow up and figure a few things out. The hardest thing was when dad was in one of his moods. The booze just made him crazier. We all had to get out of his way or pay the price. I don't ever want to be a part of anything like that."

"What were you doing before the war?" Bob said, giving Bud a chance at a happier topic.

"I was starting a junior college program in Chicago when Pearl Harbor happened. Sports is really my thing. At Hirsch High I loved football and track, and it was fun to help my teammates get better. I decided that being a PE teacher would be the best thing for me. I sure hope I get back to it soon. What about you?"

"I was trying to figure out the right career for myself too," Bob contributed. "Mom worked it out for me to attend LaSalle Academy, a private Catholic school in Providence, on a scholarship. Language came pretty easy for me. They even taught me a little of *la française* to go with the Latin and Greek. Then I was working at a factory when Pearl Harbor was attacked."

"Anybody special in your life?"

"Not lately, I've had a couple of girlfriends. There's nobody waiting. How about you?

It was an opening Bud was more than ready for.

"Well, let me show you!"

Bud smiled, reached into a pocket and produced his picture of Rosemary. Bob could see the pride and affection Bud's eyes.

"Well Bud, I'll do my best to make sure you get back to her."

A sharp observer at his best, Bob's sense of humor could be warm or cynical depending on his mood. Bud learned to accept the occasional sarcastic message. As the weeks and months went by, his own sense of purpose helped him stay steady and not react openly with hurt or anger. He learned that Bob would come around after a few hours, kind of like Bud's dad.

At the end of the third week, LeMouroux returned to check on the men. Luckily, Bud's leg had not been broken and he was now able to start traveling. Bob's burns and bruises were better too, although he had red, peeling skin and lingering pain.

"You are ready to go, but I have bad news." LeMouroux told them their planned route was dangerous but he might be able to find them a fishing boat further up the coast.

"German patrols here are thick as flies. They watch a zone several kilometers in from the sea. But we will try. My cousin to the north has a fishing boat. He doesn't like the Germans, but he is too scared so he does nothing to resist. I threatened him that if he does not help, I will tell his wife about . . . well that is not important. He agreed to help but we must go. I have a friend with a cart and he can take you to the boat. It will take a day."

"I know I keep asking," apologized Bob, "but has there been any news of anyone else from our crew?"

"Actually, M. Neil, yes. There were two men. One was caught in a tree and a German patrol found him. He was injured so they sent him to a hospital in Paris. Another landed in a cabbage field and was found by another patrol. An SS officer took him to the site of your plane and then he was shipped off."

"Do you know where they are now?"

LeMouroux looked at the ground and whispered something to Bob. Even though he could catch a few words now, Bud could not understand a conversation in the French tongue. He had not been fond of language study in school, where his attitude was, "Give me some math and let me alone."

What would happen if he got separated from Bob again? Speaking to locals could save his life.

"What did he say?"

"He said Jerries captured two and took both of them away."

At the end of the week, Carlach arrived again, this time seated behind two lean oxen pulling a farm cart loaded with hay. He was dressed in coveralls with a tattered jacket and boots. Bud and Bob, now also wearing farmhand clothes, climbed aboard and stretched their aching bodies before what they knew would be a long period of enforced stillness.

Bud looked up at the house that had sheltered them, and saw a banner painted on the stucco; *Villa Jeanne*, in a rosy glow of dawn light. *I like that name.*

Bob rubbed an ointment on his burned skin and flexed his face to keep it from scarring just as LeMouroux had told him, before climbing into the back of the cart to be covered with canvas tarps and a thick layer of hay.

"I pray when I return home, I will never visit a farm again," Bud whispered mischievously to Bob.

"I agree, this hay itches and stinks. I'm afraid I'll never feel clean," Bob quietly laughed.

Carlach called softly to his oxen and the cart began to roll, groaning and swaying down the lane. Bud and Bob did not converse, each trying to find comfort in his own thoughts. About two hours into their journey, Carlach whispered, "Keep down and keep quiet. I am approaching a *boche*." The flyers now hardly breathed.

A young German officer stood by the side of the road next to his motorcycle. Friendly and self-assured, he called out "*Bonjour, Monsieur*," as he waved Carlach and the wagon to a halt. "I am embarrassed to say, my motorbike has broken down and I must get to Plouhinec. It is just up the road. Can you help me?"

Before Carlach could answer, the man rested his hand on the Luger pistol holstered on his uniform belt, a small gesture of overweening self-confidence and power. Since the invasion, the French had learned to read these signals of dominance and work around them. It was foolhardy to ignore them, equally so to react.

"But of course, *Monsieur*," said Carlach.

As the soldier began to walk around to the back of the cart, Carlach quickly guided him to come forward. "Please sit up here with me. That hay is not fresh and has many spiders in it. Here, you can use my cushion."

Carlach pushed an old cushion across the bench for the soldier to sit on. Speaking French, he replied "Why thank you, *Monsieur* . . . ?"

"Carlach."

"Ah, such a beautiful day, Carlach, is it not?"

"*Oui, Monsieur*, this is a day to enjoy the world."

The soldier stretched out on the seat and regarded Carlach. "I was down in Gâvres a couple of days ago. A quaint little town.

The food was delicious, but such a tragedy. They were hiding some English in the attic of the inn."

"Ohh?"

"Such a tragedy. It was my favorite place to eat there. But the rules are very strict. People who help the English, Americans, Jews, Resistance, they are kaput!"

"But of course." Carlach smiled and wiped his brow.

The soldier continued as if he had not heard Carlach's response.

"Let me tell you. The Gestapo executed them. Killed them all. You must be careful, eh, Carlach?"

Carlach had a knife under his coat but he faced a trained soldier. If one of the Americans even sneezed under the hay, this man would probably kill them all. Even worse, the *boche* would find his family and kill them too. He slowly moved his left hand toward his coat.

"You know, Carlach, we are not monsters! We reward you French for helping us rid your country and the rest of Europe of these vermin and rebels. You, for instance. Would you risk your life and your family to hide some dirty, nasty English?"

He laughed and patted Carlach hard on the back. Meanwhile, under their tarps, Bud and Bob barely breathed. Bud peeked carefully through the hay at the front of the cart and briefly saw the soldier's face in profile as he sat on the seat in front of him. He looked even younger than Bud and Bob, baby-faced and blonde.

"Ah, where are my manners, *Monsieur*. Of course, you would do the right thing. Look, you have given me a ride. Why am I here talking about such dark things? You are nothing like those people in Gâvres. Look, there is Plouhinec now. I meet my patrol there in a couple hours. Will you join me for a bite and a drink, my friend?"

"I am so sorry but I must get this hay to Sainte Hélène."

Carlach did not want to reveal his true destination. The soldier might have patrols check him out later.

"I must get this hay to my sister there. Her heifer is about to have a calf and they will need the extra hay."

It was the best Carlach could come up with on the spot, but judging by the man's soft hands, he had never seen an honest day's work in his life and so would probably know nothing about farming.

"I totally understand. Who did you say your sister was?" the soldier asked in an innocent sounding voice.

"Oh, she is Claudette Chevrolet," Carlach improvised. He hoped this soldier was not a Gestapo member, who would research such responses and hunt down anyone who lied to him.

"Good, Good, M. Carlach," said the soldier with a wink.

The soldier strode up to the inn and was met at the door by two other soldiers who greeted him warmly and patted him on the back. It was obvious the three of them were looking straight at Carlach and the soldier was telling his story. The Frenchman smiled and waved and urged his oxen to hurry on.

"We must get out of this town," Carlach whispered. "Do not make a sound or move until I tell you to, *oui?*"

Bud and Bob were not about to move. They were shocked and relieved that they had not been discovered.

There was one thing that Carlach had not lied about. There were bugs in the straw. It took all the will power the men had to not scratch at the spiders, bees, beetles and ants crawling on their bodies and hair.

About half an hour later, Carlach pulled the cart off the main road. He listened for any motor vehicles. When he felt it was safe, called for the men. Bud and Bob almost jumped from the hay, scratching and slapping. They hungrily shared the bread and wine Carlach had brought for their journey.

"It will be getting dark soon. I do not want to stop anywhere before we get back to my village, Le Petit Roscoet."

"I don't care if it is dark. Just get us there, *mon ami,*" Bob said as he lit one of his cigarettes. Under the circumstances, food and drink were the top priorities, though Bud smoked a little and wondered where Bob was getting tobacco and paper.

"It's not safe to be out at night. The patrols are more likely to stop and question us if they catch us out after dark," warned Carlach. "By the way, practice how you smoke when you are here in France. Never between your fingers. Hold between your thumb and first finger like so. Watch how the French do these kinds of things so you will not be obviously American!"

Actions that were invisible to Bud would stick out like a sore thumb to the Nazis. There was a lot to learn.

"Then let's get moving," he urged, though he was not keen at getting back into the bug-infested hay. He scratched at the array of bites on his arms and legs, rubbed his sore leg and pulled himself back up on the cart. It was still far and away better than the alternative, he thought, crawling back under the hay. It had been dark for an hour by the time they reached Le Petit Roscoet. They were at another small farm. In the deepening shadows he saw a face approaching them that he recognized. Eagerly, he climbed down from the cart.

"Welcome, M. James," said Bassereau, who had been in the car that took them to Saint-Pierre-Quiberon. "M. Diabat sends his regrets. Since you left, the *boche* searched his farm again and threatened him and his family. His son was questioned. They even took Mathurin away for a few days of rough treatment. He would only speak Breton, and that made further questioning seem not so useful. He was in bad shape when they dumped him back at his home. He didn't care. He never told about you."

"We can't thank you enough for your help and all the risks you and your friends are taking for us," Bud said. It seemed like so little to offer.

"It is we who appreciate you," responded Bassereau. "You come across the ocean and risk your own lives to help save *la République*. We despise the *boche* invaders and will fight to the death with General de Gaulle to lead us on."

Not for the first or last time, Bud felt deep appreciation. These people had families, but risked their lives and the welfare of those they loved to help him and other airmen trying to get to safety. He hoped he could return someday and properly thank them.

Chapter 6

Helper Heroes

Photographs: for forged identity cards, since photos are almost impossible to obtain in German controlled lands, because possession of a camera is a legal offense on the continent. Civilian clothes, correct size: (1.3 x 1.4) neutral gray background. Should be full face, head and shoulders, no hat. Insist on having three copies along on every mission. Above all, keep them clean and un-creased.
—Classified escape and evasion instructions

From the first day they parachuted into France, Bud and Bob relied on raw courage, sheer luck, divine providence and human kindness. Walking from town to town, they risked encountering Nazi sympathizers, informants and many too scared to help an Allied airman. German patrols prowled the countryside hunting for evaders like the two Americans and anyone who helped them.

Many times, under the care of well-connected citizens or underground members, Bud and Bob were not informed about where they were going next. They were put in a cart or a car and taken to a home where a family would protect and care for them. Other times, they would walk up to 20 miles through the night to find their next hideout on their own.

They could now pose more easily as French citizens. Their tattered clothing helped them blend into the local population. New documents had taken time to produce while their identities were verified. The Resistance knew Nazis sometimes jumped from planes and posed as downed Allied flyers to infiltrate and destroy Resistance networks. When detected, these impostor flyers had short lifespans.

James Wilschke identity photo 1943.

Robert Neil 1943.

"You shall know me from now on as Jean-Marie Roussack," Bud declared proudly, showing off his new identity card.

"Pleased to meet you, M. Roussack. My name is Yves LeMere," Bob replied.

Bud admired Bob's new identification card in return. Using the photographs of themselves in civilian clothing each man had kept from their survival kit, Carlach had his contacts prepare documents that looked properly aged and authentic. "Now we have to remember who we and each other really are."

"You do resemble a fellow I used to know, name of Neil, but that was a long time ago."

Most of Bud and Bob's helpers were ordinary people unconnected to any organized Resistance movement. They all had one thing in common; because they despised the Nazis, they were willing to gamble their lives to help the Allied forces. It grated on them to watch the occupiers seize property and impose their will in all things. Those expressions of tyranny inspired the French to never relent.

In addition to these citizens, some organized Resistance groups formed escape and evasion lines that were committed to rescuing American and British airmen, hiding them, feeding them, tending to their wounds and sending them back to their units in England. Each region also had its own *Maquis* (rural guerilla fighters) resistance networks, working to sabotage German military units, supply lines and operations. Some groups were expert at assassination, especially targeting Gestapo and local French collaborators. Despite not having the best rifles, Resistance fighters were able to pick off German soldiers with a bullet from afar, or use explosives to disrupt or sabotage factories and rail lines.

Underground groups carefully communicated and cooperated with one another when possible, moving fighters, weapons, ammunition, forged documents, supplies and, most importantly, information across and around enemy lines. At the same time, it was important to not share too much, never revealing real identities. The Nazis were skilled at torture so the less information someone knew, the better.

Ordinary German soldiers sometimes seemed to feel a bit of compassion for the people they had occupied, but many Nazis, such as members of the German Police and the Gestapo, were cunning, methodical, and merciless. They would coerce the local populations while tempting them with cash awards for turning in Allied airmen. Women and children were deported to German prison camps. French citizens faced cruel decisions to inform on the Resistance or see people they loved tortured or killed. People suspected of being Jewish, communists or saboteurs were exiled to unknown destinations never to be seen again. Men were sent to work in German factories where they became ill and died.

Leaving Quiberon in early June, Carlach helped the men travel to Petit Roscoet, a farming village, where they stayed with the Joannic family, hidden in a trench in the woods. Eight-year-old Simone Joannic enjoyed the dangerous adventure of helping shelter the airmen. As a part of their disguise, Bud and Bob carried Simone on their shoulders, pretending to be her mute uncles. The family snuck them food at night, and in a gesture of caring and courage, Simone and her mother slipped carefully through the dark to bring them some of her First Communion celebration dinner and the special Breton cake her mother made for her, a rare treat in wartime.

When they could, the "uncles" worked in the fields to help the families who supported them. When a car full of German soldiers pulled up alongside the field one morning and seemed like they were about to come over and talk to Bob, who seemed by all appearances a young farm laborer, he thought fast and reached for his pants zipper, quickly heading for the edge of the woods adjoining the field, pulling his pants down as he walked to make it look like he urgently needed to attend the call of nature. Perhaps disgusted, the Germans spoke briefly with the French farmers and then left, leaving Bob alone, with his pants down and his heart pounding.

As often happened, after about a week, their host family worried that a neighbor might be suspicious and it was time to move again.

In mid-June they moved to Guernehy and the Carnac farm, a short walk up a country lane from Petit Roscoet. Staying in the family's attic, they could look out a small round window at the road and the family's lane, keeping an eye out for unwelcome visitors. A specialty of Brittany, cider grown in the family's apple orchard made their stay sweeter.

The two safely bounced from home to home, field to field, barn to barn, but whenever they got close to the seacoast and the possibility of salvation, they encountered German patrols. Wearing civilian clothes and carrying false documents, they were in danger of being executed as spies.

Operating "in disguise" was especially dangerous for downed American airmen who wandered near airfields or military compounds. The Germans used many excuses to save themselves the trouble of sending captured men to POW camps, where they were treated poorly but still at a cost to the German war effort. Flyers were among the most highly trained soldiers and the enemy was determined to prevent them from getting back into the war.

Fortunately, Bob's improving French had proved instrumental in getting through a couple of close calls.

Early in their trek, the danger to the Americans and their helpers was dramatized by a British flyer who called himself Mark. Fluent in French, he had Resistance connections and wanted to help as many evaders get back to England as possible. Mark promised Bud and Bob that he would find them a boat to get them back across the Channel. Days went by without word and the men wondered what had happened. Word came back to them through the villagers sheltering them that a British man had been caught and buried alive for espionage.

Bud and Bob learned a lot on the road, increasing their ability to find their own resources and helpers. The task was made more difficult because at all times they had to rely solely on their memories, never writing down names or speaking about their French friends to others.

Throughout, there was physical discomfort. Feet and clothes were more often wet than dry. The ever-present bugs were as hungry as Bud and Bob were and left plenty of bites and scabs. The two men were usually unwashed, but they tried to keep up their grooming to look less like they were on the run.

The Eighth Air Force anticipated that their downed crew members would find themselves in enemy territory where, in order to evade capture, they would need and could expect to a degree, support from local people. Airmen were trained to approach isolated farmhouses that did not look well kept, making sure there were no antenna wires to be seen. Paid by the Germans to help them, collaborators were likely to have better-outfitted houses. The best might have been requisitioned by the Germans to house their own troops. "Evaders" were taught to identify themselves and hope they would be fed and possibly connected with resources to escape the country. They were told that anyone who turned them away might have good reason. They should just move on without attempting to persuade reluctant residents to become hosts. They were told always to be humble, approaching a farmer to ask if they could spend the night in the barn or another outbuilding. Even though the men were hungry, they learned not to ask for food right away, because the answer would usually be "*non*." If they were lucky enough to be allowed to stay, the farmer would often offer them a meal or two, even though food was often scarce for their own families.

In late June, walking through the countryside alone in the early evening, the two pilgrims approached a home that looked promising. Tired and hungry after a long hike, they were not thinking clearly. As Bob felt more confident in his French skills, he walked up in the fading light and confidently knocked on the door. Bud stood behind watching, anxiously awaiting the response. As soon as the door opened, Bob felt shock and dismay. Three German officers were just feet away, eating at the farmer's table.

Bob caught his breath and thought fast. He looked in the eyes of the farmer and spoke quietly. "Hello, pardon me, *Monsieur*, my cart has a broken wheel. Do you know a place we might stay until morning when we can fix it?"

The farmer looked at them with knowing and nervous eyes.

"No, I apologize, but I already have guests."

One of the officers was curious. He set his glass down and pushed back his chair.

"*Oui*, but of course," Bob said quickly. "*Merci.*"

The farmer distracted the officer with another bottle of wine as the vagrant visitors moved out of sight into the twilight.

That night they slept in a field of thick grass away from the road in case the Germans came hunting. That near-miss taught them to watch who went in and out of a building for a long time before approaching a home or business.

Chapter 7

The Dreanos of Trelecan

To the best of my recollection, we stayed with
27 families during our 6-month stay.
—Bud Wilschke

Food was more plentiful in the country, where they could eat fruit and vegetables from the fields they traversed. Yet, it was easier to hide in a city, where strangers were less unusual. Their helpers sometimes let them stay in upper floors of a house where they could be more comfortable, but they always felt the threat of discovery and the risk of being trapped. Sometimes there was little or no food. Occasionally they were able to eat well, depending on what resources their hosts had available. In their honor, their hosts would sometimes toast them with a special bottle they had been saving for the celebration when the reviled *boche* were finally driven from their homeland.

For months now, Bob and Bud had been on the run, moving among a series of attics, churches, and sheds, always a step or two ahead of being betrayed or discovered. If they encountered German soldiers— and they did on a few occasions—they were cautioned to take a cue from several of their helpers and use the phrase, "*Je suis breton*," meaning "I am from Brittany and speak Breton." This implied that they did not speak French, German or any common language. Some Germans spoke French but few spoke the Celtic-based Breton. The ploy worked more than once.

Bud and Bob 1943.

As they walked or bicycled across the countryside from village to village, the open air and blue skies, verdant fields and rolling hillsides made the young Americans homesick. The way home was not yet clear. Moving steadily from place to place, it seemed they traveled in large circles around Brittany, no closer to finding a way out of the country.

In mid-June 1943, the two travelers made it to the village of Trelecan, where they were sheltered by the Dreano family until mid-July, moving between the attic of Dreano's cabinet shop and a small church just across the road. M. Dreano was a friend of the church caretaker, who lived in a home next to the church.

Bud and Bob often had to carefully crawl into small attic spaces. Once inside, they would be cramped and cold at night and sweating in stifling heat during the day. This time they climbed into the attic of the church in Trelecan, pulling a cleverly disguised trapdoor up behind them so that it was not visible from below.

That night, Bob struck a match to light a candle to see his way in the dark, cramped space.

"Is that safe?" asked Bud. Normally, they lived much of their lives in darkness.

"I can't even see the nose on my face. Just this once, let's have a little light so I don't feel like a trapped mouse under the floorboards."

"It only takes one bit of bad luck."

"We've got a candle and the means to light it. Devil be damned!"

Apparently, his declaration to the devil was, in some quarters, a call to action. Next door, the caretaker's five-year-old daughter saw the light from her bedroom window.

"Father! Look at the window! Satan is trying to damage the church!"

Her father kept secret radio equipment to help the underground, and knew he had to act fast. "*Oui, ma petite*, I will take care of it immediately."

Her mother reassured her that Satan would never be able to move into the church, while her father hurried to scold the men. The next night, he moved them to Dreano's shop.

There was too much risk to the family for the men to stay in the shop for long, so on about the third day the Americans were moved to the attic of Chapelle Sainte-Brigitte–Landévant, a partially-abandoned remote country church. Surrounded by fields, the little chapel-like church was sheltered by a grove of trees. Its condition suggested that it was rarely visited. The Dreanos' teenage son, Antoine, rode his bicycle to bring them meals and was eager to practice his English with the *"Aviateurs américains."* Eager to become a teacher, he offered to trade some practical French phrases, as well as a few choice colloquialisms, in exchange for their advice on approaches in English to appeal to the fairer sex.

Antoine started with Lesson #1 by writing *Comment ça va?*

"This means 'How's it going?'"

Bud repeated the phrase but pronounced it as the English word "comment" and was bewildered to hear the French pronunciation *'como.'* Antoine decided it was better to teach them spoken rather than written French. Proper spelling was not needed in most situations they would encounter and bad pronunciation could give them away in one utterance. They could expect to be questioned at the train station by German police who would try to trick evaders by speaking in French initially and then tossing in a last-minute English phrase like "Have a good trip." If an American instinctively turned and responded with a thank you, he would be arrested on the spot.

"'How far to town?' is said like this: '*A quelle distance de la ville?*'"

"How much is the bread? *Combien coute le pain?*"

"Can you give me a ride? *Pouvez-vous me donner un tour.*"

"When is the next train? *Quand est le prochain train?*"

"I need your help, please. *J'ai besoin de votre aide, s'il vous plaît.*"

Just for fun, Antoine slipped in a few less practical yet in his mind essential phrases:

"Where do I find dancing ladies? *Ou puis-je trouver des dames de danse?*"

"You are very beautiful! *Vous etes tres belle!*"

"Will you keep me warm tonight? *Voulez-vous me garder au chaud ce soir?*"

Bob had already improved his conversational skills and pronunciation, so while Bud focused mainly on learning the words, Bob polished his accent. Their instruction and conversation with Antoine helped pass the tedious hours in hiding. They enjoyed his wit and youthful exuberance despite the wartime challenges. Antoine had no doubt that the war would end, the Allies would win and France would be liberated. After that, he was sure there were many young women waiting to meet him.

"*American jeunes filles*, they are *belle, non*?"

"*Oui, bien sur!*" replied Bob. "American girls are pretty. And they find Frenchmen to be very good-looking. After we win the war, I'm sure more American tourists will want to visit France, including girls your age."

"Americans have all kinds of sayings too. Here's one for you, Antoine. 'I'm still buying green bananas,'" Bud smiled as he quipped.

"*Qu'est-ce que cela?*" What does that mean?

"I expect to survive long enough to eat the bananas!"

Bud imagined Antoine dreaming of newfound possibilities and his image of America as he dropped the attic door behind him. Antoine was a fun-loving companion and host, but the flyers wanted to move on closer to the coast. Every day the answer was the same: "I am sorry, *Messieurs*, not today. It is not safe yet."

A week had gone by in the church attic and Bob thought he would lose his mind with boredom. Even with a good traveling companion and fellow airman at his side, Bob was weary of the uncertainty. He couldn't look forward by setting goals on the calendar because he had no idea where he might be the very next day. Bob prided himself on his strategic life decisions, but in this situation, he had to trust others he didn't even know. Every moment was anxious. He could never tell how close the Germans were to detecting his presence and possibly executing him on the spot.

Bud had the advantage of being able to step out of their musty loft and into daydreams of Rosemary. He could hear Cab Calloway's "Call of the Jitterbug" as he swung Rosemary in dance, one weighted step for every two beats of music rhythm. He imagined making the rounds of local Chicago clubs with his intended, celebrating the blessed end of the war. Cramped in his current physical reality, his imagination gave him a way to stretch his legs. Like finding the energy to climb a mountain by imagining himself at the top, Bud looked into a bright future of love and family. The war with

Germany was just a bump in the road. His future with Rosemary kept Bud climbing his wartime mountain.

Bob and Bud also built homecoming stories to pass the time and to visualize setting foot on American soil once more. They kept their spirits higher by spilling out hopes of a better future for the world and for themselves, sharing images and lighting up the darkness of their captivity. They imagined the joy their countrymen would feel when the war was won. Bud could see the jubilant fireworks shooting above Lake Shore Drive and over the waters of Lake Michigan. They told stories of happy childhood memories that they looked forward to replaying with their own children.

And of course, they thought and talked about how to get back home. Their efforts to that point had gone nowhere.

One afternoon, restless from their cramped hideaway, his muscles aching for challenge, Bud showed off to Bob how he could do handstands and handsprings, landing lightly on his feet.

"It's easy enough. Just make your movements smooth, and spring at the right moment, bounce right up. I did these all the time." Bud's powerful arms and shoulders seemed like they could bounce him across a road as he stood balanced on his hands and then flipped backwards to land upright on his feet.

"Most impressive, Bud, but be careful not to go through the floor."

Bob was not so sure he had the right balance to try this trick. Then he looked around their current lair in disgust. Bud's fooling around had stirred up clouds of dust. The dark corners and ceiling were covered in thick spidery cobwebs. It was not the most perilous place they had stayed, but there were no windows in the attic, only the cracks between the boards on the outside wall, and the air was stale and still. There was nothing to look at, no way to watch what was happening outside their diminutive world. Even as they talked, they had to keep their voices to a whisper. Even the most insignificant mistake could spell disaster.

Finally, Bob couldn't stand it another minute.

"Bud, I'm going stir crazy. Just lying in the dirt is making my skin crawl. I'm going for that broom downstairs. At least I can sweep a space for you and me to sleep."

"Well Bob, if that helps you settle down, go for it." Bud was able to peer through cracks in the wall of the church attic. "Let me keep an eye out for anyone moving in the field." It looked safe enough.

Bob lifted the trapdoor, lowered a ladder, clambered down into the church and brought the old broom up. He pulled up the ladder up behind him and lowered the door. He swept quickly and, he hoped, quietly, to clear the thickest cobwebs. The spiders had to hustle out of his way. Small rays of sunshine lit beams of swirling dust.

Bud was amused, knowing that his friend would feel a little better when his space was that much cleaner and neater. At times as the men traveled together, he worried about Bob. He fell into dark moods, quiet for hours at a time, with a faraway look. In this moment, anyway, Bob seemed cheerful, happily sweeping away. It was good to have some control, however superficial, over their lives.

In their focus on the task at hand, the men forgot to keep watch. Before he could return the broom, the two heard someone come into the church. Bob carefully cracked open the attic door and peered down below.

"Oh Jesus and Mary, save us," Bud's heart pounded.

From Bob's point of view, it could have been a witch. He saw an older woman, scarf wrapped around her head and wooden shoes on her feet, begin bustling underneath him. She unwrapped her head scarf and put down her bag. She looked around, back and forth across the church. He could hear her moving objects around and muttering to herself. Suddenly, she let out a frantic scream, crossed herself quickly and ran from the church, leaving her belongings behind.

Bob didn't know whether to laugh or cry.

Later that day, Antoine came to see the two men. He was not his normally cheerful self.

"I am sorry *Messieurs*, but we will have to move you tonight. Today Mme. Belle, a volunteer parishioner, came to clean the church. It was not her regular day or I would have warned you. She looked for her broom but it was not where she expected it. She looked all around and couldn't find it. Very little changes in her world. This was a big deal. She thought there might be bandits or ghosts here, so she ran all the way back to town, telling everyone that something evil was in the church. Nobody usually listens to her crazy stories, but we can't take the chance that someone might come to investigate."

"Bandits or ghosts?" Bob choked on a laugh. "What did she think they needed a broom for?"

Bud nudged him with his elbow, but even he was about to laugh.

"Thank you so much for helping us. We'll get ready," said Bud.

The young man saluted them and gave each of them a hug. They were going to miss Antoine, but they still had to find a way out of their larger confinement, the entire occupied country of France.

Chapter 8

Collaborators and Betrayal

*Security—once his organized journey has begun, the evader will
never mention to the various helpers to whom he may be handed,
the names of his previous helpers or the methods used by them.
He will NOT—on any account—write down the names or
addresses of those who have helped him. If arrested when in the
hands of an organization, he will refuse to give names or other
clues and will refuse to identify any helpers who may have been
arrested at the same time.*
—Classified escape and evasion instructions

By early July 1943, the Americans, Bud and Bob, were moved to
Nantes with the aid of M. Noël Bredoux. A mechanic with a Talbot
car and motorcycles, Bredoux was well-connected and able to bring
food and documents to airmen who were evading capture, and often
moved them himself. He had access to gasoline and black market
links with another young townsman, M. Jean Chanvrin. In his job
working for the local police, Chanvrin was able to supply forged documents critical to the Resistance. Because of this position of trust, he
easily learned about area Resistance operations and personnel.

By July 20, Bud and Bob were sheltered by Mme. Jeanne
Sebastien, a school principal, and her 16 year-old daughter, Mlle.
Francine 'Mimi' Sébastien, who both worked for a Resistance group
known as Marie-Odile. After their stay with the Sébastiens, Bud and
Bob each stayed with Chanvrin, and then at another home.

However, the maelstrom of war often led to dreadful choices,
and it was rarely clear whom to trust. Unknown to the Sébastiens,
Chanvrin was arrested in September 1943, when he betrayed his
countrymen and women. Perhaps because his own family had been
threatened, as he later described, he revealed the names of several
Resistance members. He tried explaining his stance to his girlfriend
when she realized he was an informant.

"We need to survive, first and foremost, and that means being on the side of those in power. My mother and father are in danger. They may be tortured or die in prison. We are trapped in a war we didn't create and we have the right to take care of ourselves the best we can."

"But Jean," she argued, "even a mention of your visits with the German colonel will cast suspicion on you and your name will be despised long after the war. Your family will be destroyed."

"We don't know what will happen or who will win or when it will be over," Chanvrin replied. "We can't afford to stand up to the Germans right now. I will tell no one about the Gestapo's awareness of local maquis activities. I will be protected as a friendly informant and they will remember my help after the war."

Chanvrin did not heed his girlfriend's warnings. Some even believed that his arrest was staged to mislead other Resistance members. Shortly after he was detained, mass arrests of Resistance members followed. He betrayed two different Resistance groups, Liberation Nord, specializing in intelligence, and Marie-Odile, specializing in helping evaders. In doing so, he betrayed Bredoux and the Sébastiens to the Nantes Gestapo. Released soon after his arrest, he is believed to have remained employed by the Gestapo, even serving as a driver for their officers.

Mme. Jeanne Sébastien was arrested and deported to the notorious Ravensbruck concentration camp for women and then imprisoned near Paris, tried for treason, tortured and sentenced to death. On the eve of her execution, Paris was liberated and she was released to the Swedish consulate.

Bredoux fled from Nantes, disguised as a priest, but was arrested in December 1943. He was sent to two different prisons before being deported to Buchenwald, another of the largest SS concentration camps. Bredoux survived.

Bud and Bob may have never been so close to capture as when they were in Nantes. It is virtually certain that Chavrin did not betray them only because it did not suit the larger purpose of infiltrating Resistance networks.

Chapter 9

Deep Resistance

We talked it over and decided that Wilschke would do the map reading and I would take care of the food. We were like two foxes playing hide and seek with the hounds. I got food everywhere. Some from farms, some was given. In the country there were plenty of eats, and good, too. People who had been saving Scotch and brandy for after the war would treat us. This made us figure that even war has its compensations.
—Bob Neil

For the next several weeks, Bud and Bob bounced around several places in east Brittany. In late July, they were spirited to the Manoir de la Chaussée of Mme. Marie Moquet and hidden in a remote attic for two nights. The two then were moved on to a fishing hut along a river towpath near Châteaubriant, south of Rennes, by M. Boscherel, a butcher from Langon. "You should be safe. The *boche* here are lazy and do not walk along the path. They like to stay on the other side of the river, where the road is good. Do you like to fish? I will bring a net and you can help me stock my shop with fish."

"I love to fish!" said Bud, with eagerness. "I used to do it all the time in the Chicago River."

On a late summer afternoon, Bud and Bob were seining. Stripped to their skivvies, each took an end of the net and waded out into the cool flowing water. They moved in broad arcs to capture a mix of carp, trout, and salmon. Most of these would go to Boscherel's butcher shop to sell to the locals but Bud and Bob knew how to make a tasty meal, too. Focused on fishing, the war briefly seemed far away. Then Bob looked up and felt a wave of shock. Several German soldiers were piling out of a car on the other side of the river and it looked like they were stripping down to bathe. They were casually joking and obviously not on duty.

"Bud, don't turn around. We have company. Let's keep moving downstream and let them have their fun."

Nodding to the Germans, the Americans casually grabbed their clothes and fish and faded into the woods. After that escapade, they stayed in a small hotel on the river for three or four days, more careful about their movements.

In early August 1943, M. André Huertier, a pharmacist from Rennes, helped Bud and Bob move to the home of Mlle. Andrée Récipon, a trouser-wearing, chain-smoking, serious-minded nurse. She had served heroically in World War I and then moved back to live on the beautifully forested but run-down family estate she had inherited, the Château de'Laillé. Récipon belonged to the Liberation Nord Resistance group. She sheltered and helped create false documents for evaders, refugees, and army deserters fleeing enforced service of the Germans.

Mlle. Récipon knew it would be too dangerous for Bud and Bob to stay in the house. Raids were common and there was much at stake. Instead they hid and slept in a dugout in the dirt far into the woods from the Château, camouflaged by branches. They bathed in a pond nearby, the water black with decayed leaves and mud.

Récipon and Abbé Held, the escaped Assistant Archbishop of Strasbourg who was hiding out at the Chateau posing as a local priest, worked out a system to allow Bud and Bob and other airmen a measure of freedom to move about in the forest.

"James and Robert," Récipon told them, "just watch the Father as he strolls the property. He will hold his prayer book in front of him. When it is safe for you to move about, he will keep the book open as he walks. But if you see it closed, you must hide immediately!"

A Polish grocer named Marian Wilke, another of Récipon's refugees, regularly brought food to the dugout home. Wilke had been conscripted into the Wehrmacht after Germany invaded Poland but escaped and found his way to Château de'Laillé. Because of his limited, heavily accented French, he was given the identity of "Roger the Mute."

The forests around the Château were rich with wild game and the men were well fed during their stay. However, the hunt was also attractive to the Germans. One day, Wilke, tending the horses, was terrified to see several large cars pull up to the Château. He immediately moved behind the barn and raced to the woods. From the windows of her Château, high above the surrounding community and forest, Récipon thought this was the raid she knew might come. She watched the Germans coming from a distance but waited in her home until a group of officers knocked on her massive oak front doors. She greeted them warmly.

"*Bonjour, Messieurs*, welcome to my home. What brings you here today?"

A highly decorated officer spoke for the group. "*Bonjour*, Mlle. Récipon. We have been admiring your woods and wonder if you would allow us the privilege of hunting here." The officer's correct form of address to Récipon indicated that he knew something about her. Not too much, she hoped.

"But of course, gentlemen," she replied. "But please let me tell you how to make the most of the experience."

She proceeded to delay them with an elaborate description of the property and the game they might find, while Wilke raced into the woods to warn Bud and Bob to hide. They moved quickly into their dugout and covered it with a camouflage of brush. Then, as they had done many times, they sat quietly in the dark, dank-smelling earth, waiting for a signal that it was again safe to come out. They listened intently to the sounds of the forest and heard gunshots in the distance, hoping they were from hunters and not soldiers fighting or even executing their allies.

"Yeouw!"

The calm of the dugout was suddenly shattered as a wild boar, fleeing the hunters, charged through the brush. Looking for any place to hide, it thrust his tusks and snout into the dugout, and tried to wedge itself in.

Bud stifled a yell. "You get out of here!"

He grabbed a shovel they had used to build the dugout and, with little room to swing, slammed it at the big boar's snout as hard as he could. Bob, bringing up the rear, threw rocks but was unable even to shout for fear of alerting the Nazis hunting nearby. The shovel struck again and again until the bloodied swine staggered off. It was hours before the Americans stopped trembling.

Later, when the Germans had departed and the airmen were able to describe what had happened, Récipon laughed and prepared an excellent ham dinner that night.

"Poetic justice," she told them. She described her own disgust at having to talk to the Nazis. "I swore to God I would never speak to those *boche* swine again!"

Raised Catholic, Bud and Bob were both able to enjoy Abbé Held's ministry and to take sacraments from him while they stayed at the Château. They eagerly joined the effort to build an altar hewn from timber they cut in the Château woods in a clearing surrounded by large fir trees. Récipon draped the altar with white linens and adorned it with boughs of greenery. Despite the risk of a raid, on August 12, 1943, they all took part in the first Mass the Archbishop conducted there. Wind instruments and violins played pieces by Bach, Beethoven, Handel, Stradella and Fauré.

Récipon, Wilke, friends and other Resistance attended. Bud, on his knees, was the first to receive communion. At the end of

Fifth from left Mlle. Récipon; sixth from left Abbé Held; ninth from left James Wilschke, tenth from left Robert Neil

Bud and Bob with Mlle. Récipon.

the service, Abbé Held blessed and gave rosaries to each evader to carry on their quests. Récipon served the faithful a celebratory lunch, and they sang *La Marseillaise* and the Polish national anthem. The legendary event, which came to be known as The Mass of the Maquis, was photographed and written about in underground newspapers, building morale for the Resistance.

Not long after that first Mass, Récipon arranged for the Americans to be moved further along on their exhausting journey. Because she knew the Gestapo was watching her every move, she did not reveal to the next helpers who she was or where the two airmen had originated.

Bud at communion.

Chapter 10

Trapped in the Mill

Once evasion and/or escape has begun, a person involved must discard his true identity, both in appearance and behavior. He must adopt in every particular the attributes, clothing, and manners of the inhabitants, among whom he will have to travel in his journey back.
—Classified escape and evasion instructions

Bud and Bob kept moving, but they were constantly frustrated in their plans. It was too dangerous to go near the coast and they were still circling around Brittany. Although they had not been captured, they felt trapped in France.

Leaving Récipon's Château in mid-August 1943, they were guided by helpers to Bédée, about 20 miles northwest. There, they had the good fortune to be sheltered by another leader of the underground, Félix Jouan. Decorated for his bravery fighting the Germans in World War I, Jouan had been an outspoken leader in the community. A short jovial man with a mustache, he and his wife Marie-Louise owned a farm and built a large flour mill in the village. Prominent and well-liked, his breads and pastries further built his name. After France was invaded in 1940, he helped organize several Resistance networks, including Liberation Nord. He frequently sheltered English and American flyers. As part of the Resistance, however, he needed to be quiet about his opinions.

Bud, Bob, and Félix Jouan 1943.

For about two weeks, Bud and Bob were hidden in a barn on the Jouan farm. The men were happy to help Félix, Marie-Louise, and their children, who were about the same age as Bud and Bob. The Americans loved working outside but had to stay out of sight.

After a few days in the fields, Jouan drove them into town in his van to help him in the mill. He was standing behind the bakery counter about mid-morning when he saw a German officer's car pull up in front of the building, swastika flags flying on both front fenders. Jouan waved at his wife to hurry Bud and Bob to the top level of their six-story building. The men each dove into a corner stacked with supplies, pulling tarps over themselves. Once again, they were listening in the dark, hearts pounding.

Downstairs, the Commandant and his soldiers swung the door open and strode in, crowding into the bakery space and staring at Jouan.

"M. Félix Jouan," the German commandant announced, looking at the baker with piercing eyes, "The Reich needs new headquarters. You will immediately make your mill available to us until further notice." The officer was accustomed to people accepting whatever he told them. This situation could be no different.

"*Ah, oui*, Commandant," Jouan replied. He knew how to bide his time.

Even as the commandant spoke, trucks pulled up. Troops spilled out and quickly moved office materials, boxes of documents, furniture and communication equipment into the bakery building. Outside, two soldiers set up a radio antenna. They clearly intended to stay for a while.

Jouan had no choice but to accept the invasion. Over the next days, he worked his bakery business around the presence of the soldiers. He gave them food and hospitality while he considered his options.

Bud and Bob were trapped on the top floor in the August heat, sweating and feeling smothered under tarps covering lumber and grain sacks, where an occasional rodent eyed them curiously. Overhearing the activity below, they feared that a German soldier could walk up to their floor at any moment and see them or sense their presence. Like stowaways they were cramped and unable to move for hours.

It was even difficult for Jouan to signal to Bud and Bob that he had not forgotten them. He had to sneak them food and water at odd hours. Sleep was impossible as the risk of discovery grew.

Jouan finally came up with a desperate plan to help the men. He sent a message for his most closely trusted friend to visit him. The two Frenchmen stepped outside in the August sunshine.

"Louis, I need your help with a dangerous mission. We have to sneak these Americans out of here. Have Gérard and Paul bring the truck with 50 sacks of wheat."

That night, Jouan took advantage of a moment when there were no Germans in his building and sprinted up the stairs.

"*Mes amis*, we are getting you out tomorrow. In the morning, two men will haul a large load of wheat up here. Be ready to swap clothes with them and walk out and into my truck. Keep your eyes down, hats low and pay no attention to anyone else."

Bud and Bob, cramped and aching from lack of exercise, were eager to follow his directions. "If we get out of this place alive, I will thank my lucky stars," Bob whispered. "I have never felt so trapped."

The old, heavily laden truck wheezed up early the next morning with Louis at the wheel. Two sturdy farm hands riding in the back with the wheat got out and walked purposefully up the five flights of stairs, a large sack of wheat on one shoulder, again and again. They gradually emptied the truck, careful not to draw attention to themselves, never looking in the face of any soldiers. Over the course of the morning delivery, they became part of the background to the Germans.

Jouan, meanwhile, did his best to ensure the soldiers were comfortable, amused, and fed with his best pastries. The mill ground on as usual in the lower level, filling the air with noise and a haze of flour dust, while the Nazi soldiers stayed busy with their paperwork. Staff cars pulled up with materials and messages. Soldiers strode in, clicking boots and giving Nazi salutes. This microcosm of the Nazi war machine operated parallel to M. Jouan's bakery and his clandestine activities. He observed the Germans closely too. Information about their methods and habits would help the Resistance strike back.

As soon as the last sacks of grain were settled in the top-floor storeroom, the two laborers quickly swapped clothing with Bud and Bob, who pulled on caps, boots, and sweaty clothes. They took several deep breaths and casually shuffled down the stairs, showing fatigue with every aching movement. Past the blank stares of the soldiers, they wound their way through the crowded rooms. Within moments they were outside in the bright sunshine. They climbed into the waiting truck, careful not to look excited or vigorous. Louis was ready and wasted no time pulling away from the mill and down the street.

Later that day, Jouan fed the soldiers and had other workers come into the mill. On the way out, Gérard and Paul joined the group and slipped away without notice. Astounded at their near miss, Bud and Bob soon moved on toward Rennes.

Chapter 11

Friendly Fire

Salient factors [for evasion and survival] are: luck, adequate and repeated briefing, common sense, knowledge of terrain, good feet, patience, ingenuity, determination, and stamina. The very fact that you've gotten as far as this room would seem to indicate that you all possess these qualities.
—Classified escape and evasion instructions

Leaving Jouan, the Americans returned to Rennes, where they again spent an afternoon in the care of André and Mme. Heurtie. They were driven back to Châteaubriant and hosted by M. Pierre Troudec, M. Marcel Letertre, and M. Bernard DuBois. Then they were driven to Saint-Julien-de-Vouvantes and sheltered by M. Robert Monin.

Every day was a challenge, but they were weary of the endless effort without a breakthrough. Yet again unable to reach the coast, they returned to Nantes in September, where they stayed with M. Eugène and Mme. Germaine Langlet, Jean Chauvrin (the informant), M. Pierre Mauge, M. Jean Ligonday and Mme. Suzanne Clement, who described herself to them as "your mother in France."

An important city on the Loire River, Nantes is about 30 miles east of the Atlantic coast, the depth of the German coastal defense zones in which the Nazis were especially vigilant. Any further west from Nantes toward the sea, they would run into increasingly intense scrutiny and security.

In Nantes, Bud and Bob stayed in relatively comfortable apartments at times but were not free to travel about the city. No one seemed to have a clear way for them to find their way to the coast or to get to Spain.

Their favorite accommodations came with radios. The German occupation could not seize all the receivers in France but forbade listening to broadcasts from England. All across the occupied and

Vichy France, people secretly listened to stories of the Allies' fight to take back the continent. To them, the BBC broadcast messages of hope and inspiration, information about battles and coded messages about secret operations.

Bud and Bob were especially eager to hear news and music that reminded them of home. Bud was a fan of Frank Sinatra, a new star that he knew Rosemary would enjoy, hearing with personal significance Sinatra's hit, "People Will Say We're in Love." Bob loved "That Old Black Magic" by big band trumpeter Harry James. They were cheered by the progress of the war, concerned for their fellow soldiers and anxious about what would happen next, particularly to them.

They had a right to be worried.

Late on the afternoon of Sept. 16, 1943, in their apartment hideout above a bistro a quarter mile from the center of Nantes and close to the river harbor, the undercover Americans heard a familiar rumbling in the air.

Bud listened carefully.

"Sounds like our boys. Wonder where they're headed?"

He and Bob moved toward the forbidden window.

"Looks like a big run, probably over a hundred '17s."

"I hear some Thunderbolts up there too, ripping it up," Bob observed of the dogfights that appeared so chaotic from the ground.

Within a minute, they were surprised to hear flak exploding in the air and feel the vibrations of the bomber engines and propellers. They could hear the sharper-edged roar of the German fighters, and the rattle of machine guns from both sides. Waves of bombers were targeting the port where subs and ships had been moved for safety.

The darkening sky was lit with thousands of big and small flashes of high explosives. Air raid sirens screamed. Their apartment building shuddered. Dust and plaster fell from the ceiling. From the windows, they could see buildings in the center of the city and near the river crumble and go up in flames.

To counter the attack, German defenses blasted away and sent up a smokescreen to hide factories where the Nazis were making war materials. The air was thick and acrid, the noise deafening. Bud and Bob hoped for the best for their colleagues in the bombers. It was too late to move to an air raid shelter even if they had wanted to. They crossed their fingers for accurate targeting of the bombs so they would fall away from the civilian zones like the one where they were trapped inside.

"I hope those guys tuned up their Nordens," bombardier Bud breathed.

The beleaguered flyers rode it out, counting on luck and the skill of their comrades, as the raid went on for almost half an hour. All the city's utilities were disrupted and they later learned that more than 900 civilians died in that raid. Still, their contacts said that most French understood that the Americans were trying to do the right thing.

A week later, by the morning of September 23, gas, electricity and water were finally restored. Just as life seemed to be limping to normal, another big raid began. B-17s and flak again filled the sky above. Flames, smoke and dust filled the air below as Nantes' industrial and port facilities were destroyed. This time, Bud and Bob heard the sirens, saw what was coming, and fled their hideaway for shelter outside the city. Pulling a couple of abandoned bicycles out of the rubble, they moved quickly across the broken streets of the crumbling city. Looking back, they saw another wave of bombers come behind them, the second raid of the day for Nantes. They were in the countryside by nightfall.

In total, more than 1,700 people died in the Nantes raids. More than 2,000 buildings were destroyed. The French people were not afraid to take casualties but public opinion shifted for a while after so much civilian death and destruction.

After 120 days of dodging Nazis and being on the run, they were convinced that escape by sea was impossible. It was time to take their chances to escape in the opposite direction, to Spain.

Chapter 12

A Truly Narrow Escape

General Behavior. Never forget to show gratitude to your helpers no matter how little they are able to do. Always try to remember (without writing it down) the names of your helpers, but never try to get in touch with them at a later date in order to thank them or tell them of your safe arrival.
—Classified escape and evasion instructions

Walking and biking south the American flyers covered about 250 miles by mid-October. They had been seeking a way home for about five months. They hunkered down for two weeks in the city of Tulle, staying with a series of three farm families who were part of the underground. A picturesque, mid-sized city in a rugged part of central France, a river flowed through the center of Tulle between steep stone bluffs bounding the north and south sides.

There were only two ways to come in and out of the city, along the route of the Corrèze River valley and between the bluffs. This did not seem unusual or risky to Bud and Bob when they arrived. Wary and alert, they still appreciated a brief respite while they figured out their next steps to get back to England.

A long way from any place they wanted to go, Tulle could be considered *en route* toward the Mediterranean. The city was a hotbed of the Maquis, who repeatedly attacked German troops and supplies, stole weapons and explosives and assassinated Gestapo and their collaborators. The Gestapo became more determined to crush them.

In Tulle, the flyers again stayed with M. Eugène and Mme. Germaine Langlet and two or three other families in the area. One night they hid in a small barn loft back of the Langlet property at the outer edge of the city. Behind the barn was the steep bluff that ran the length of Tulle, where the Langlets planted grapes up the side of the ravine.

As he brought a supper out to their barn hideout on their first evening, Langlet set his best bottle of vintage cognac on the table. "I was saving this for the end of the war, James and Robert, but I want to toast you and the American people!"

Though Bud was normally not an enthusiastic card player, while they were in hiding, he and Bob played to pass the time and bet to see who would cook or clean up the evening meal. Sitting together in the dim light of their hideaway quietly playing poker, they heard footsteps rushing up the back steps toward the room where they were hiding. They stopped the game and listened intently with quickened pulse. This was not how their host typically moved through his property. M. Langlet suddenly entered the loft of the barn through the door in the floor, breathing hard.

"The *boche* have sealed up the city-- It's a roust! They blocked the roads out of town, and patrols are hunting Resistance. They are at the house now—we must get you out. Go where we showed you before. Quickly!"

Always prepared to move at a moment's notice, Bud and Bob grabbed their coats and small bags. Quietly leaping down the stairs and running towards the back of the barn, they heard loud banging and shouts in German.

Langlet silently motioned for them to follow him to a small door he had shown them earlier in case they had to get out fast. They squeezed out within seconds and crouched low, following a deep ditch. Langlet closed the door behind them and hurried back into his home to await the raid and stall the soldiers. Bud and Bob could see flashlight beams darting in all directions around the farm. Men were shouting and dogs were baying. Once again they were hunted by the Gestapo.

Creeping in the dark, they climbed up a sloping hill through rows of vines at the back of the farm, pressing close to the bluff. A low-slung crescent moon was covered by clouds, the deepening darkness easing their escape into the hills. On their own, they headed out of Tulle.

Chapter 13

Hunger Dreams

We posed as everybody and everything except what we actually were. I finally wound up with a fancy zoot suit outfit. Bet I could have won a prize as the best-dressed refugee in Occupied Europe. It sure took a sharp eye for anybody to know I was an American in that outfit.
—Bob Neil

Never leave any leftover food on your plate. It is an unwritten crime, and would be sure to attract attention.
—Classified escape and evasion instructions

Escaping from Tulle in mid-October 1943, the downed American flyers, Bud Wilschke and Bob Neil, found themselves moving through central France. On their own again without contacts or connections to any Resistance or underground network, they hiked in the dark through the fields and woods along the Corrèze River valley from Tulle to Brive-la-Gaillarde, about 20 miles. There they again found safety with the Langlets and had a chance to change their wardrobe.

"What do you think?" Bob asked Bud, strutting around in his new finery.

American flyers were typically larger physically than their French counterparts, and their feet were bigger, too, so when this time the suit fit he decided to wear it. It was a zoot suit, a 1940s style for a night on the town, designed to impress the ladies, with a high-waist, tapered trousers and a long, exaggerated jacket with padded shoulders. It would be his outfit for the next few weeks.

"You look ridiculous!" Bud laughed as he laced up his boots.

"But do I look like a soldier on the run?"

"No, you don't look like any soldier I know. You look like you're ready to go dancing."

The last few weeks had been difficult, moving from house to house, chased out of Tulle, walking through fields in the dark from town to town, always fearing discovery. They had been lucky so far, but for how long? The stress weighed on them both but Bob seemed to be more hopeless lately. Bud was glad to hear him joking around.

"Just because we're running for our lives, doesn't mean we can't do it in style," Bob grinned as he did a quick twirl on the heel of his shoe, a cigarette hanging jauntily from his lips. And while the shoes were not a great fit, they were the best he had worn in months, with smooth, dark leather and no holes in the soles.

"Seriously though Bob, what are we going to do now? We've been hiding out for months, and France is sticky as a tar ball. It's been a long while since we had a good meal. I'm dreaming about food constantly. It's like I'm always smelling the burgers and fries I used to cook. When my friends came into the Miner-Dunn restaurant, I made food that made them swoon. I can smell it. I can taste it. A little salt and butter, a hot grill, ground beef medium rare, buns toasted just right. Crispy, fresh-cut French fries with ketchup! And then a big malt, chocolate! I'd walk ten miles right now for a bite. No, I'd even walk that far on my knees."

Bob was just as happy for the diversion a food fantasy could bring.

"Yeah, I've been dreaming about the meals my mom used to make, really vivid dreams. We ate a lot of potatoes, but oh boy, could she make chowder. Beuuutiful! Rhode Island style, onions! Bacon! Potatoes! She would make her own broth. All down the block, people would come for just a sniff."

Bud looked dreamily into the distance. "My family's chickens meant we had the best eggs, and Mom would roast a hen on Sundays when she could. She would make soup the next day with carrots and onions from the back garden and we would be living—

Bob returned to his theme.

"We had corn cakes and clam cakes, the best ever. Now, I want to be back in Joe's Tavern, drinking a Schlitz and eating one of his wiener sandwiches with a pretty girl at my side."

Bob turned to Bud with conviction — "Let's head to Spain and get there as soon as we can. We can't wait any longer, the weather will get colder in the mountains."

Their old plan was close to dead. Crossing the German fortifications on the coast and then making it across the sea was daunting, Bud agreed. It probably wasn't going to happen.

On the other hand, many of their contacts had warned them it was not safe to cross the Pyrenees, but it increasingly looked like the only way home. They were hungry, gaunt, tired, and working to keep hope alive.

"Langlet said there are even more patrols on all the escape routes into Spain. The terrain is all but impassable in some areas," Bud said. "But what choice do we really have? The last time we had any contact with underground helpers was a week ago. I think you're right, we have to go now, or we may never make it out of France. It'll be POW time for you and me, and Uncle Sam will be too busy to come help us out."

"Right. I don't think we should try to pass through the central mountains though," Bob continued. "We don't have the proper gear and we'd need a guide. It's going to be snowing there soon, and there's no way we could get through the high mountain passes. I think we should head here," he said, pointing to the Mediterranean coastline in the southeastern part of France on his well-worn silk map. It had saved them a number of times. By now they knew the country well.

"Perpignan? I suppose you're right, but that's a long trek."

The Eighth Air Force evasion manual, Bud remembered, had suggested Perpignan as a route for evaders.

"That's why I have my dancing shoes on."

Bob grinned as he tapped the toe of his black and white patent leather loafer.

"I'm going to dance all the way there."

Chapter 14

Closer to the Pyrenees

Approach the farmer when there is no one else around and tell him who you are. Ignorance of the language is no drawback: everybody in Europe knows the R.A.F.; an American is slightly less known.—The phrase Je suis américain is sufficient.
—Classified escape and evasion instructions

As autumn deepened toward the coming European winter, it was colder and there was less food to scavenge in the fields and orchards. They often had to sleep outside, and Bob's fancy suit was not keeping him warm.

Bud was working on a plan.

"Look here on the map, let's get to Narbonne and then head to Perpignan and Rivesaltes. It's just north of the Spanish border."

"How are we getting to Narbonne? That could take us another week or more from here."

"We have some cash. We can get train tickets."

"Germans are watching the stations. That'll be tough."

Riding a train seemed like the most dangerous thing they could do in France. All it would take was a slightly more-suspicious-than-average Nazi to ask too many questions and not accept their Breton-speaking act.

As the sun rose on a brisk October day, the men moved carefully among the hedgerows. Seeing a local farmer coming out to tend his animals, Bob took a chance and walked toward him to call out a greeting.

"*Bonjour, Monsieur,* may I talk to you?"

M. Estève Opoul looked surprised and concerned. Even far out in the countryside, farmers worried that the Germans would come and seize their crops and send their families to work camps in Germany—or even execute them.

"We are American flyers, in need of a place to stay and rest. Can we sleep in your barn tonight?"

Opoul hesitated, looked around carefully, then led them into his barn. He pointed to his loft and soon brought them cheese, bread and fresh water from his well. The men ate eagerly and settled into the hay for a welcome sleep protected from the frost.

Bud and Bob stayed on Opoul's humble farm for a week, helping him with his chores while he made sure they had as much comfort as he could provide. Opoul discreetly asked his neighbors for options to help the flyers. No one had an idea or connection.

Bob wasn't about to give up.

"*Monsieur.* Your hospitality is beyond reproach. I must pay you for your generosity."

"No, no, it was my pleasure. I could not take any money."

Playfully, he added, "Though as farmers, you fellows just aren't worth that much!"

"Please, perhaps you and your family could use some clothes this winter," Bob persisted. "America is grateful to you for helping us."

"It was nothing, really."

"There is one more favor we would like to ask. We need train tickets to Narbonne. We will pay you for your trouble."

Bud and Bob often worked odd jobs and had been given money by other underground members. In addition, they still had francs left from the money provided in their escape and evasion kit. Bob took out a pack of francs and reached to hand it to Opoul. It was enough to pay for the tickets and a healthy commission. They had to get out of the country quickly or they would be stuck trying to survive the winter.

"*Monsieur,* the *boche* would kill me and my family if you are caught."

"I know it is a lot to ask. Please consider it. You just get us the tickets and we will do the rest."

Opoul looked at the money. Bud and Bob watched him consider briefly.

"I will help you under one condition. Don't tell my wife. I am more afraid of what she might do to me than the *boche.*"

The three men laughed. Opoul returned early the next morning with the tickets, two cloth sacks of food that Mme. Opoul had prepared and the name of their next helper, M. Jean Villeroux.

"I bought your ticket on the slow train—less likely to be watched by Gestapo. This means you will be sitting longer at the station. More time for Gestapo to see you and be curious, so you need to look like you belong. Get off at Narbonne. Any further on the train and you enter the forbidden zone, so more likely to be challenged. Then walk south. At Rivesaltes, find Villeroux. He may be able to help you."

Bud and Bob shook hands warmly with Opoul and then, walking a distance apart from each other, they followed discreetly behind his cart into town and to the train station. Opoul gave a subtle wave toward the correct train. Taking seats away from each other on the station platform, the Americans assumed their characters as Yves and Jean-Marie, weary French travelers, and waited. Each carried a French newspaper to pretend interest in.

As train announcements jangled his nerves, Bud furtively observed those around him: farmers, businesspeople, workers, soldiers, women with children and many who were more mysterious. An unknown number were, like the two Americans, not whom they seemed to be, including other evaders, escape line helpers, informants and spies. Beyond that, there were smugglers, assassins, and many others hiding their identities. Throughout the occupation, there were sudden outbursts of gunfire, chases, and bodies left on the street to send the message of who was in charge. From the Resistance side, trains were frequently sabotaged and Nazis and their collaborators shot. In occupied France, there was not much chance to relax.

Large German propaganda posters on the station walls surrounding them told a bigger story. Calling it the *German National Railway* implied that France belonged to Hitler's Fatherland. The image was a train charging out of a tunnel, high stacks billowing smoke. Another train, crossing over a rushing river, symbolized the German's ability to surmount any obstacle. More trains lined up six deep in a station showed the mass of German strength. A family—father, mother, son—stood by the side of the tracks giving the *Sieg Heil* salute to a passing train.

Other posters warned of the risks of not adhering to rules.

"You would do well to turn in traitors"

"You will be rewarded for supporting the cause"

"Join the victors and enjoy the spoils of war"

Some were more encouraging:

"Food, shells and fuel come first. If your train is late or crowded, you must not mind!"

"A new era has begun—so all aboard!"

"WAFFEN SS" in huge letters was accompanied by the image of a helmeted Nazi soldier with a stern expression, a rifle with bayonet pointed menacingly outward and a swastika banner behind him.

A shadowy face of helmeted soldier peering straight at the viewer with the caption "He's watching you."

Some were in German, suggesting that the French would soon need to understand the language:

Sieg um jeden preis. (Victory for everyone)

Others were in French to coax the locals into being collaborators:

L'Allemand est vraiment ton ami. (The German is really your friend)

Among all the propaganda meant to intimidate, Bud steadied his nerves with his mother's old saying "in for a penny, in for a pound." They were committed to a plan now and really had no way of turning back anyway.

Finally their train arrived, brakes screeching, engine huffing, steam and coal smoke swirling. Standing and stretching with their fellow passengers, they found corner seats away from each other, pulled their caps down low over their eyes and pretended to sleep the whole way to avoid conversation with anyone. Bud wondered if there were other evaders on their own journey.

The train bounced and swayed along the varied terrain. Stopping at many village stations, the trip lasted well into the following day. The battered railcar grew crowded, riders filling in the empty seats. An unusually friendly woman sat next to Bob. She greeted him and asked him where he was traveling, but a wave of the hand and a sleepy snort successfully put her off.

The 20-hour journey was a long time to pretend to sleep, while not daring to really sleep. From his seat, Bud could peer past his cap at the passing countryside and darkening night. He marveled how farms showed the passing of the day. Activities shifted as animals were cared for and bedded down. Families retired to their homes and lights went out as the night deepened.

In his enforced private reverie, Bud rehearsed the name of his contact, Jean Villeroux, now critical to his escape. He tried to imagine the hike over the Pyrenees, anticipating the ways things could go wrong. Not difficult. Even negative thoughts led to home. It had been five months since the crash. He had not been able to get any word to Rosemary—she might believe he was dead. After six months it would be official. Killed in Action. KIA.

Finally, the train screeched into Narbonne station. Stepping off, he and Bob quickly oriented themselves and moved through Nazi security checkpoints to exit the station, lucky to meet no special scrutiny. Relieved, they soon rejoined and were on their way, buoyed by their growing hunger for freedom.

Chapter 15

Dangers Near the Border

It is possible, but dangerous, to hitchhike. Cars and lorries are nearly all German and must be avoided—because only German or axis collaborationist have gasoline vehicles.
—Classified escape and evasion instructions

Off the train in early evening, the two American evaders headed south from Narbonne station. Walking through dark fields, their goal was Rivesaltes, about 38 miles away. They were close to the Mediterranean coast now and approaching the foothills of the Pyrenees, a particularly dangerous forbidden zone. The snow-capped mountain range rose in the distance to the southwest. At times the sea was visible in the distance and they could feel it in the warm breezes. On November 7, they walked down a hill toward a broad golden valley, warily approaching the city of Rivesaltes.

Moving along the edge of a field, they came to a crossroad, but realized a large black Mercedes was traveling slowly toward them. Bud saw it first.

"Bob, bad news. Let's scram!"

The men ducked, scrambled into a ditch and moved quickly away from the road. They listened as the sedan stopped and two men got out, walked around the back of the car, relieved them-selves, went back in and the car moved on.

"Wow, we were lucky to see them first," Bud exhaled. "Gestapo wagon."

The sun sunk under the horizon soon after and the men walked on, alert to danger.

"It's just down there," Bud said softly. "Rivesaltes."

There were candles in windows in the valley below and a few dim street lamps, quiet and unassuming like most of the hamlets they encountered.

"Let's keep our heads low and find a place for the night. We can find Villeroux in the morning."

Under a clear sky, the air cooled quickly once the sun went down. They made their way along the outskirts of Rivesaltes by the light of a half-moon, light enough to travel, but dim enough to hide them or so they hoped. Crossing a large field, they were startled by flashes of light followed by thunder. Bob grabbed Bud's arm.

Guns!

It was not a storm. These were muzzle flashes from very large armament. Big guns. A lot of them. Now they could smell the explosive charges from what they guessed were tank rounds. The shells screamed by and blew up the dirt a hundred yards beyond them.

"We need to hit the gas, Bud. They may not be firing at us, but those shells could kill us just the same."

Calculated by the flashes, the firing seemed to be clustered and the source was not moving. Each barrage lasted a minute or two followed by a pause for reloading.

"Ok, Bob, they take about 30 seconds to reload each time. When they do, let's run."

Bob nodded. Terrified for months, on edge every instant, his nerves were not helped by how little he had slept and eaten. Whenever Bud had mentioned that they both had lost a lot of weight, he laughed and changed the subject, but Bob clearly felt the burden of his time in France. Every day he wondered if he would die in some roadside ditch where only the buzzards would find his body. His fellow traveler was his strength when his own left him. Bud was always good for a joke, a laugh or some outrageous observation, as well as good, sober judgment.

The shelling paused again.

"Ok run!" Bud commanded.

Unfortunately, Bob was wearing his oh-so-fashionable suit and less-than-practical shoes. He had joked that if he were going to die in this God-forsaken country, he would do it in style. But now, sprinting breathlessly through the blasts, he wished he were wearing his boots. These soles had no grip and no support for his ankles as he stumbled across the rutted field, splatting in freshly spread manure but avoiding the tank rounds through luck more than any-thing. They made it to the other side of the field, gasping but thank-ful, then came to a dirt road just outside of town. Stopping to catch their breath, they drank from a pump next to a horse trough. The water was icy cold and chilled them through.

"What do you think, Buddy boy? Safe to go into Rivesaltes tonight?" Bob massaged his sore ankles and legs. Knowing he was headed for the mountains, he feared twisting his ankles as much as being hit by a shell. "This is a dangerous place so far, but now we can find a place for some food and maybe a bed tonight."

Bud's heart was still beating hard from the close call. They had been told that Rivesaltes was relatively safe. Still, walking into a French city without knowing exactly where they were going was risk-ier than many of the things they did. "Let's just bed down here under these trees," Bud advised. "We've tempted fate enough for one day,"

After so many nights of bunking rough, they were easily asleep in minutes.

At dawn they walked on, and in the early morning light they saw a lone farmer, busy moving a few sheep into a corral.

"Let's ask him for help," Bud suggested, and Bob agreed. They approached the wary stranger, introduced themselves, and asked for help finding M. Villeroux.

"Oh, that's not so difficult. He works with the mayor. He has a favorite rendezvous where we are likely to find him."

The three walked into the hamlet and found the bustling café. It was crowded with locals beginning their day. No German soldiers were to be seen. The farmer gestured toward a man seated in the corner.

"Villeroux, right over there."

Their latest friend went out the door on his way. The Americans approached the table where Villeroux was sitting alone, perusing the local paper.

"*Pardon*, Monsieur Jean Villeroux?"

Villeroux appeared deep in thought, then a little unsettled by the question. He scrutinized the two men.

"*Oui*, and you are?"

"My name is Bob and this is my friend Bud. We were sent by M. Opoul."

Bob motioned to the empty chairs.

"May we join you?"

"*Mais oui.*"

Villeroux nodded and gestured to the waiter.

"Simon, please bring two coffees and croissants."

They were quiet for a moment, assessing each other across the table.

"What brings you to our fine little town?" asked Villeroux.

"M. Opoul said you were someone we should know," said Bob as he carefully watched the man's response.

"Yes I see. Where are you staying tonight?" asked Villeroux.

"We hoped to find a room upstairs."

"Oh, no, no that will not do. M. Opoul's friends are my friends too. Please enjoy your meal. I must leave to have your room prepared. I will be back shortly and we will go to M. Olibo's home. This café...some of the Germans like to come here at night. Not the safest place for you at that time, you see?"

As Villeroux stood, Bob looked at Bud and nodded. On the road together, they had learned to communicate whole conversations with a mere nod or a raised eyebrow.

"If it is not an inconvenience, we would love to accept your generous offer."

With a smile, Villeroux said, "There, it is done. Don't leave until you try some of Simon's rhubarb tart. You'll see what paradise is like. I will meet with you soon."

Villeroux pulled on his coat and black wool beret and was out the door.

Their latest helper was correct about one thing for sure. The tart was the best the two hungry hoboes had ever tasted. Rosemary would have loved the sweet-sour pastry, Bud thought, and would probably ask for the recipe. Did she believe he was still alive after all this time? Would she wait for him?

Bud and Bob spent the afternoon in a small apartment, waiting for Villeroux to return. In addition to arrangements for the flyers' lodging, Villeroux continued his preparations for plans that would be of great importance.

Nearly midnight, under a glorious span of stars, they arrived at the estate of M. Jean Olibo, Villeroux's employer and secretary to the mayor of Rivesaltes. Olibo supported Villeroux's efforts. Both were connected to several Resistance and escape and evasion networks.

"I came to work for M. Olibo as a young man," Villeroux explained as they sipped cognac by an oversized fireplace. "Both my parents have passed, and I am glad for it. Their hearts would grieve to see the *boche* invaders fouling our country like rats. Which route did you take into town? You probably traveled across some of M. Olibo's land."

"Funny story about that. There's this valley north of town." said Bud. "Not the friendliest way into town. We were nearly blown to smithereens. What was that about?"

Villeroux laughed. "Hah! The *boche* have confiscated much of our land. That area is now their firing range. The more worried they get about the Allies, more they blow things up. You are lucky they did not use you for targets."

That explained the shelling. Bob and Bud laughed hard at their mix of bad and good luck.

"Our country once proudly valued the freedom of men. Since *les Nazis* invaded us, many gave up to hide behind the devil's power. *Collaborateurs*, cowards, *traitres*. Some are eager to betray France, to be rich even if their France is no more. They want pleasure when courage is needed. Some buckle under fear. Some stand and fight, like you.

"Now, you want to make the trek through the mountains to escape back to your units. Well gentlemen, you are in luck. In about a week there is a caravan leaving Perpignan. There are other soldiers and refugees planning to travel together, led by a guide. The road is not easy my friends, and many have died trying to cross.

"There was an escape route further west across the Pyrenees operating out of Paris, infiltrated by a man using the name Jean Desoubrie. Because of him the Gestapo sent over 130 flyers to POW camps before he was exposed and we sent him to Hell. I will try to make sure that does not happen to you. We are setting up a fresh escape line. We have Spanish guides, old smugglers, but they hate the *boche*. I have personally been a part of developing the route and selecting the guides. Once you reach Vilajuïga in Spain, our contacts will help you get to your people."

The personable Villeroux was clearly part of an elaborate system. While much of the French Resistance movement was focused on fighting the German occupation with sabotage and assassination, Villeroux worked for one of the separate underground escape lines focused on getting Allied airmen and soldiers to England, where most of them had been based. American and British intelligence systems MI9 and MIS-X supported these enterprises with money and information. Planners handled logistics and found "helpers," couriers transmitted messages and safe houses were maintained to stage the groups. Underground members handed downed Allied flyers from one to another, shepherding them onto the proper trains and getting them off at the proper stops, then delivering the men to the next agent.

At the border, other helpers gathered the fugitives and prepared them for their hike. Clandestine escape routes across the mountains were devised based on German troop movements, weather patterns, availability of local shepherds who knew the terrain, and the number of escapees needing to be trafficked. Shepherds' huts dotted the landscape on both sides of the border and served as shelter for escapees.

Villeroux's line was the first real connection with an escape route for Bud and Bob. They entered the system at the tail end of their journey but in time to greatly benefit.

The Americans stayed in Olibo's home for the next eight days. It was a safe and comfortable place to rest and let their bodies recover from previous strains. Simon, the café owner, prepared their meals as they stored up energy for the hike across the mountains. Bob was thankfully given better shoes. Even though clothing was now scarce, they replaced his zoot suit with a warmer, less "stylish" ensemble for the arduous trek.

More nervous as each day passed, Bud worried about what would happen even if they made it over the mountains. Would the Spanish police catch them and send them back into the war, or would he be able to return home? What would it be like to return to the States? Would he get a job? Stay in the Army? He was not sure how he would cope. Would he have to make more bombing runs? He was not sure he could stand to ever fly in a plane again. Bob surely felt much the same.

On the night of their departure, the men stood in the dark behind the house. "You will meet Pierre at the vineyard and he will prepare you for your travels. I wish you both the best of luck," Villeroux encouraged them as he kissed each man on both cheeks and embraced them. "May God watch over you both."

Chapter 16

Snow and Nazis

*The best guides are to be found among the smugglers, whose
starting points for the journey over the mountains are
the small villages in the foothills.*

*You must be prepared to pay heavily for the smuggling services
of a guide. If you have no money left, give a
chit—it will be honored.*

*An unfit man among the party making its way over this last and
most difficult leg of the journey is, to say the least, an encumbrance.
Before this trip, the evader may have to spend many days in
hiding; therefore he must exercise—even though cooped up
in small places —as much as he can.*
—Classified escape and evasion instructions

On November 15 1943, Bud and Bob's winding six-month odyssey
across the varied terrain of France reached a critical point. Villeroux
had arranged for them to travel by car to in the seaside resort city
of Perpignan, where they would meet Pierre, a French helper, their
guides, and the rest of the escapers. It was a do-or-die decision to
join the caravan and once more test their mettle to reach for freedom. Bud felt as if the angels had erased the road behind them. This
trek could be the one to get them home. He thought back to his
high school track and field races and the satisfaction of breaking the
finish line tape, the cheers of the football crowd as he made a play.
Now he had to run for his life and trust that Rosemary was waiting
for him on the other side of this alpine gauntlet.

As the sun set behind the hills, they reached a barn nearly hidden
in a grove of olive trees. It was abandoned, but not empty. Inside the
dim barn were Pierre, two Catalan guides, a few Allied airmen, and
an array of tattered refugees ready to make the journey. Frenchmen

and Jews often sought to cross the mountains into Spain to escape conscription, persecution and deportation to concentration camps.

A short, lean, dark-haired man asked if they were Americans. He introduced himself as Flight Officer David Prosser, a B-17 navigator. Standing next to him was another American airman, Staff Sergeant Willard McLain.

Bob and Bud shook hands with Prosser and McLain and they talked excitedly about news from home and their parallel adventures in the war. Prosser, from Chicago, told how he went to Canada and joined the RAF. After the U.S. got in the fight he enlisted with the U.S. Army Air Forces.

"On our way to Romilly-sur-Seine on September 3rd, our group was attacked by FW 190s," Prosser told them. "Shot us up badly. We abandoned our plane and left it to crash near Aulnoy. I bailed at about 20,000 feet and opened my chute at maybe ten—landed in a field, bashed my ankle and all of a sudden was surrounded by curious locals."

Knowing the Germans would systematically scour the nearby landscape when they found a parachute, Prosser, who had the forethought to carry an English-French dictionary, used his limited French to ask the locals to hide his chute. Two villagers who took pride in helping downed flyers took him to a small country house.

"The farm family had little money and no connections with the underground. So, after ten days to let my ankle heal, I decided to ride my luck and set out on my own. The wife packed a sack of bread, cheese, nuts and raisins for me and I took a train to Nevers, where my helpers had told me that I could connect with the Resistance."

"Quite a feeling stepping off into the unknown, isn't it?" Bud said. "We know it well by now."

"Yes! But the tip was inaccurate —Nevers was crawling with Nazis. I was lucky to meet a Maquis fighter who arranged the next leg of my journey. I was sheltered in Nevers until September 15, laying low under the noses of the Jerries. The underground then snuck me out to Paris. Finally, they put me on a train to here."

"And what about you?" Bob asked McLain, another airman.

"I was ball-turret gunner of a B-17, the Black Ghost. Heading home from a run on Stuttgart on September 6th, a little shot up already, we were shot up a bunch more and bailed out near Beauvais. Landed in a plowed field, wandered a bit to find my bearings. Ran into a woodcutter who told me there were Krauts to the northeast. Off I went in the opposite direction and spent the night in a barn.

"The farmer gave me civvies and a pitchfork so I could pass easier as a farmer. Resistance got me to a house where I could recover and he gave me some papers. Two weeks later, I was on trains, shifted around like a pawn on a chessboard and finally to Paris. Didn't know how long the game would go on, but oh boy, I was lucky to find the French who helped me. I owe them my life for sure."

The fellow trekkers also included radio operator Guy Marulli de Barletta and bombardier France Delorie, American flyers in spite of their European heritages, both shot down the month before and just arrived from Paris by train. Unknown to de Barletta and Delorie, Prosser and McLain happened to take the same train to Perpignan.

In addition to the six Allied airmen, nine Frenchmen joined the journey. Several were Jewish Parisians escaping certain persecution, two were French soldiers who had escaped POW camps and two others were escapees from forced labor in German factories. One was a professor from Toulouse, targeted for his teaching of "*liberté, egalité, fraternité.*" Another was an avowed Communist, something Nazis could no more tolerate than being an ethnic Jew. There was talk of a Roma family joining them but the "Travelers" evidently were captured.

Bud and Bob, Prosser and McLain and their new companions naturally felt both excitement and fear about what lay ahead. This could be the last leg of their journey through hostile territory. On the other hand, French helpers had often warned them that the Pyrenees range, 300 miles of mountains with peaks up to 11,000 feet, was a dangerous method of escape.

The Eastern Pyrenees had been home to rugged Catalan people for thousands of years. Long before World War II, webs of smuggler trails spread across the range, and black market trade flourished. Now these obscure routes were a means of escape from the Nazis.

By the end of the war, several underground escape networks led thousands of refugees and escapees out of occupied France.

Their injuries, erratic diet and long miles on the road meant that despite the vigor of their youth, most of the company were not in top physical shape and their stamina was diminished. Still, they were brave men and soldiers, and the snow-clad peaks were not enough to keep them from reaching for freedom in Spain. There was nothing to do but go forward; there certainly was no better way back home.

"Pray, do your best, and don't worry," Bud remembered his mother had often advised him when he was facing a difficult challenge as a kid. He took a deep breath and looked up at the dusky mountain silhouettes outside the barn.

Pierre, an older man in wire-rim glasses, a worn suit and the ever-present beret, was a French member of the escape line Villeroux had helped build. Pierre introduced the two Spanish guides, Felip and Bruno, who would take them across the mountains. The Spaniards looked stealthy and rugged as the hills themselves, their skin weathered as their leather capes and boots. They looked like they knew the way.

Felip, tall, lean, with a narrow, wizened face and gray beard, silently observed, smoking as he leaned against a post. Bruno, the lead guide, was a short wiry fellow with a thick mustache who spoke a little English. *Un homme d'une intégrité absolue*, he mainly spoke with eyes and gestures, fierce when the group forgot themselves at times as they walked over the next days. Pierre explained to the group that they would be traveling by night, and had to be completely quiet. Not even a cough. No sound whatsoever. Bruno's glance signaled that he would enforce this command.

Pierre scowled at two young Frenchmen carrying two battered suitcases each. "You will regret those bags. It's difficult enough to cross these mountains."

The youths protested. "This is all we own. Without it, we will be penniless. We are strong enough to make it across these hills with our arms full. We will prove that to you."

"If you are so eager to die, go ahead," warned Pierre. "It will crush you as you climb. Others have said the same and you will see their discarded cases along the way. Sometimes you will see their bones." Even one climber who couldn't keep the pace put the entire group at risk. "If you endanger the group, these guides will throw them over a cliff for you and maybe throw you with them."

Pierre turned to the American airmen. "They would be like a stray cow away from the herd. If the *boche* find one of them, they'll hunt down the rest of you. Help the others if they fall. You have to move as one, fast through the night or you will be seen in daylight. Stay together and keep moving. Always keep moving."

Shoes were exchanged for rope-soled espadrille sandals, three pairs for each hiker. Bud was surprised to be told to wear them. They looked flimsy and the worst for both worlds, hot and uncomfortable until higher elevations, where they would be cold and uncomfortable. The Catalan guides favored the way the sandals suppressed the sound of footsteps and gave better grip than leather soles on the sandy, rubble-strewn mountains.

Pierre warned the group to stay off any roads and follow all instructions. The mountains swarmed with German patrols, well-armed, equipped and trained. It would be a tough journey for all of the travelers but Bud and Bob were conditioned to eating little and traveling with stealth.

At about 9 p.m., November 15, 1943, the group moved out of the barn and on their way. Bud looked ahead to see where their path would begin. In a valley now lit by early moonlight, he could see scattered stone cottages, vineyards, edges of a nearby forest and the lights of small villages in the distance. *Here we go! Time to keep my thoughts to myself and follow Pierre's directions to stay silent. Let's get through this.*

Over the climb, he and Bob supported each other with glances and pats on the back, but said little.

I hope my shirts and jacket keep me from freezing to death up there, Bob thought, looking at the shadowed peaks in the far distance. At least his jacket was wool.

The group walked southwest through fields and vineyards toward the foothills. In single file, they skirted the edges of gently rolling fields to blend in with the dark greenery of adjacent trees.

They clung close to rows of grapevines and used them to guide their way, camouflage in the ghostly moonlight. Hours passed as they went by farmhouses and tiny hamlets, avoiding places with any sign of human activity.

Through most of the first night, the elevation changed slowly and the hikers hoped their journey might be easy. By 3 a.m., the terrain shifted to foothills spread with low, shrubby bushes in thick, random patterns. The trekkers stayed away from the well-worn paths they could see leading into the distance. Every step took careful effort, feet slipping constantly on the sand, pebbles, and small stones, often slick with rain. Mile after mile they scrambled up and down rocky terrain. By 4 a.m., they were climbing steadily.

Further south, circling low peaks, they could glimpse the Mediterranean to the east, moon reflecting on the calm water. Moving along a jutting cliff, Bob heard the sound of tinkling bells and noticed slow-moving shadows in the darkness just below them. He cautiously looked down over the edge of the trail. *Some alert by a villager or even a German patrol?* His alarm turned to relief when he recognized the shapes of cows in the mountain pasture just below, a few of them moving on the moonlit slopes.

Bud could hear his heart beating now, his breath getting deeper. In the shadowy dark, he could barely see the ground in front of him. Other hikers were dim shadows. Owls hooted and bats chirped and swooped around him. The determined escapers were careful to follow Pierre's warning to silence.

At the top of a hill, a farm dog suddenly sounded a vicious alarm and Bud's heart leapt with fear. The angry barking echoed in the darkness for endless minutes. The hikers were certain German soldiers were racing to investigate, fingers on their triggers. Quickly, they got past the farm and the dog gave up trying to break his chain to attack the intruders.

Through the dark night, their guides led them through narrow openings and trails invisible to outsiders. Climbing through trees, brush and then snow, they were silent as they could be. The tension was constant, nerve-wracking, exhausting. The farther they went, the colder the weather and rougher the terrain. Once in the foothills, Felip traveled up to 500 yards ahead of the group, scouting for danger. Moving stealthily across dangerously open areas, he signaled back by the glow of his cigarette, one glow to wait and lie low. Two glows meant safe to travel further. Rounding the top of a hill and at the edge of a road, Bruno saw the cigarette glow only once and silently signaled the group. Everyone dropped to the ground. Even as they shivered, they laid still as possible, motionless for over fifteen minutes as they heard a German patrol pass nearby.

Ice on the trail froze hard and the mountain winds grew stronger, gusting over 60 mph, bending the trees around them. Climbing in single file above and then back below the tree line, they strained to keep up with Bruno, the lead guide, sure-footed as a mountain goat. Even as the climbers sweated from exertion, their street clothes and sandals couldn't keep them warm. Bud's legs and feet ached and he had to command them to move. His lungs burned and his head throbbed from fatigue, exertion and thinning air. *Don't give up, Bud.* He kept his eyes moving, scanning the ground in front of him, watching the trekkers walking ahead of him and checking on the men at the back. At times he heard them grunt as they stumbled.

At the edge of streams, they sometimes stopped to take off their rope shoes and socks, walking barefoot on beds of sharp rocks with feet that were already numb. Their legs were drenched by icy water. At least they would have a moment to sit to put their socks and sandals back on. If there were stones to step across, Bruno kept them moving as their fatigue grew deeper. It became hard to think. Their distorted senses slipped into dreams. Throats were parched. Between streams, the thirsty troop even knelt briefly to lap up thin layers of snow on the rocks around them.

Bruno offered rare, brief breaks for the trekkers to huddle under low bushes to catch their breath. These pauses were never enough for them to feel ready for more climbing. The less-fit would barely catch up before Bruno started the march once more. The young Frenchmen staggered under the weight of their valises but still gripped them. Bruno frowned but made no demand.

Masters of the terrain, the guides knew how far they had to move before stopping for the day. As progress was slow, they kept the men hiking two hours past dawn, finally beyond the foothills and up into steeper terrain. Topping one peak, they caught their breath as they sat to watch the sunrise and admire the Mediterranean shimmering in the distance.

The rising sun promised warmth, but resting in the sunshine made them visible to German outposts and patrols. Instead, Bruno herded the group into a ravine, hiding them from the Germans but from the sun as well. Their bodies cooled and their muscles stiffened as they huddled under low branches. They ate from their rations and did their best to find comfort on the rocky slope.

The exhausted troop had been silent but now, during the day's rest, they talked in soft voices and heard stories from their fellow travelers of narrow escapes from the Nazis and aid from the Resistance and helpers they had met. They made informal bets about the end of the war, complained about their aching bodies, and wondered what to do once they reached Spain—how to be repatriated or find a place to settle in until the war's end.

Bruno accepted some of the chatter. When it began to get louder he signaled that they were making too much noise and the men again were quiet.

I wasn't this cold even at 27,000 feet, Bud thought as he shivered. *Boy, that flight jacket I left with Diabat would be the thing to keep me warm right now. I suppose I'll never see it again.*

As ever, his imagination was his best escape from discomfort. Here he was, it would seem, actually on the way out of France. If he were lucky, in a day or two he could be back in England. In another week, back in Chicago. Picturing Rosemary's cozy home and feeling her arms warm around him, the chill of the mountains faded.

His reverie was interrupted by tense voices from some of his fellow hikers. One of them, ignoring the danger of German patrols, complained loudly about his painful feet. He sounded hopeless and agitated.

Bruno sharply drew his finger across his throat to demand silence.

The hiker persisted.

While Bud observed with alarm and contemplated his next

move, Bob crawled over and leaned toward the dangerous belly-acher, saying something Bud couldn't hear. Bud thought he might have been encouraging him in his despair or maybe he threatened to kill him. It didn't matter. The man relented, no Germans came, no one died at that moment, and the sun marched across the gap between the mountains.

Finally, the daylight faded into evening. It was time to coax their aching bodies to strive again. Bud was amused to hear the quiet moans, feeling the pain himself.

Limping and frozen stiff at first, their muscles slowly warmed up enough to regain some strength. The climb was sharply steeper now, usually up but sometimes down a slope into a valley. Past the tree line, the snow was deeper. Bud scooped fistfuls of icy crystals to his mouth as he walked.

Reserves of energy were waning but Bruno's gaze pressed the men beyond their limits. Trudging through wet heavy snow to his knees, one of the young Frenchmen staggered, tumbled, and laid trembling and exhausted. Bud, Bob, and the other flyers took turns supporting both of the young men after that, but, as had been predicted, the valises stayed behind.

Climbing along cliff edges, they crouched on narrow, snowy, slippery paths. Rivers rushed below through vast expanses of jagged rock. One slip would end a life. Each man moved cautiously, grasping at tree roots to keep from trembling and losing his footing.

Moving down a cliff, Paul, one of the Frenchmen, slipped and fell headlong into a fast-moving stream. Bathed by the icy rushing water, he lay stunned, exhausted, and gasping from the shocking cold. Bud watched him stand and stagger out of the stream bed, drenched and shivering. Despite his extra bad fortune, he found his footing, remembered his purpose and kept moving. The only way to not freeze to death was to keep walking. Complaining wouldn't keep him warm.

A stone shepherd's hut, hidden from the trail, brought the hikers to a pause. Bruno allowed those with cigarettes to smoke inside the hut so no telltale glow would be visible to German spyglasses. Others sat outside on a narrow stone wall circling the hut. The group somehow managed to come up with a dry shirt and sweater for Paul so he could continue in the miserable state that had come to pass for comfort. Catching their breath, they looked out at the moonlit valleys below.

In the steeper reaches it was more difficult to move without being seen. Climbing through one pass, Bud was startled to see a searchlight probing from the sky, sweeping a valley below them. *What in the world is that, the Second Coming?*

Bombs fell on the valley floor and explosions echoed for several minutes, probably another example of German target practice. They hoped it was not an attack on a group like theirs.

Near the border, German outposts were often strategically placed in old outposts or fortresses, watching the valleys and hillsides for evaders. Snipers and machine gun posts menaced anyone moving toward the border. Even with Felip scouting ahead, at one point the hikers were shocked by an intense searchlight suddenly blazing across the trail, throwing shadows against the mountain. The company hit the ground and barely breathed as the searchlight swept over their still forms. Apparently, they didn't look much different than the rocks.

About 3 a.m. the second night, climbing to a large, high altitude plateau, Bud was startled to see they were within 200 yards of an old stone fortress perched just above their path. A searchlight probed from a small tower, sweeping the plateau, searching for targets. In the dim red glow of the sentry's station, he could see silhouettes of German soldiers with rifles and machine guns. *If I can see them, they can see me. How are we going to get by this one?*

He could see about a mile of deep snow stretching ahead on the high plateau.

We'll be a cinch to spot, slogging through that snow. Sitting ducks for snipers.

With little alternative, the group was determined to try to get by. Spaced out in single file they moved toward the open expanse, crawling on hands and knees, when a sudden snow squall swept over them. Recognizing opportunity, Bruno held them back until snow filled the air like fog and blinded the searchlight. Then he waved them to run across the plateau under the cover of the storm.

"Run. If you stay here, you die. If you make it across, freedom is yours."

Bruno sprinted ahead, breaking a trail in the snow. Every step seemed to take all the energy they had. Two men staggered, stuck in snow to their waists, exhausted and despairing. Bud and Bob pushed their way back to them, wrapped their arms around the men's shoulders and pushed themselves and the struggling comrades forward, as if straining to reach the finish line.

"Come on boys, we've got this. Turn up the gas! Do it for the folks back home!"

They somehow found the energy to keep pushing, step after step. The swirling blizzard filled their tracks and the sentries saw nothing.

Within an hour beyond the plateau, Bruno slackened his pace, turned, and looked Bud in the eye. His smile was surprising.

"Tell the men to watch for lights past the ridge in front of them. In the next valley you will see Spain."

Chapter 17

New Dangers in Spain

If about to be taken into custody in Spain, try to give yourself up to the military, and avoid both the Special Police and Civil Guards.

Guardia Civile can be spotted on platforms by the tricorne, or triangular Napoleonic type of hat he wears. Keep out of his sight by getting off the train on the side opposite the platform, only getting on again as it starts to leave the station.

Do not carry foreign currency into Spain, except at your own risk. The act is punishable by up to nine months as a civil offense.
—Classified escape and evasion instructions

Descending through pine and then into oak forest and the warmer air of dry Spanish foothills, Bud, Bob, the guides, and their fellow escapees rested for a few hours. Gradually their bodies warmed, their spirits soared and they felt safer than in many months. The group cautiously walked down into the tiny village of Vilajuïga, reaching town by early morning. The guides took their French *francs*, gave them Spanish *pesetas* in exchange and vanished. Bud and Bob, Prosser and McLain needed to get to the American consulate in Madrid. They walked into the village first.

Bud noticed villagers begin their daily routines, a little curious about the wretched-looking refugees. They spotted the smoke and steam of an old train just pulling into the station and quickly made plans to try for the next one that stopped.

The airmen strategized briefly and decided to buy tickets in groups of two, hoping to attract less attention. They walked along a narrow street to the tiny train station, where Bud and Bob approached the ticket counter. While their French was limited, their Spanish was even more meager. Bob did his best, speaking French, English and pantomime, trying to negotiate their trip.

"*Un momento, señor,*" said the clerk behind the counter, avoiding Bob's eyes. He waved for them to wait at the far end of the room, turned his back and spoke excitedly into a primitive, dilapidated telephone. *This could be bad.* The would-be train riders were tempted to break and run but within minutes, several Spanish police in dusty blue uniforms, leather three-cornered hats and bandoliers surrounded them, menacing them with battered World War I-era rifles.

A brief glance between Bud and Bob signaled that they would not try to flee *el policía.* Bud's newfound and hard-fought sense of freedom evaporated into the dry Spanish air. They had evaded the Germans for months only to be arrested by the Spanish *Guardia Civil.*

The Americans were rounded up and herded to the local police station. The guards there were more relaxed, genially offering cigarettes and making attempts to show sympathy for their plight. The police chief shot some perfunctory questions in Spanish at the group. The police searched the men and recorded their names but, given the language difference, could do little else. One guard grew bored, set his gun against the wall, and shared tips on rolling a good cigarette. A savory meal of rabbit, rice and tomatoes from the local café arrived in an iron pot, and the famished men relaxed a bit. Things didn't look too bad.

Eventually, orders came to the local police about how to handle the refugees. More clumsy than aggressive, the officers bound the men's hands and shoved them into a decrepit railcar on the next train.

Arriving in the town of Figueres about an hour later, they were loaded into the back of a decrepit truck. In the early evening darkness, they bounced along rutted roads south until they reached a sprawling, centuries-old stone fortress, where they crossed over a stagnant, muddy moat and entered through a large iron gate. The police waved them out and pointed down the hall. Past a heavy wooden door, the group entered a reception hall dominated by a large painting of Generalissimo Francisco Franco.

Despite the call from the jailer, the escapees were not expected. They waited into the evening and were finally interrogated by an intelligence officer and his young interpreter. They were quizzed about their escape and from which French town they had arrived. The American flyers offered only their name, rank and serial number. Annoyed and disdainful, their inquisitor threatened them with deportation back to France, but they were not hurt.

Bud and Bob were led into a large tiled room for a cold shower. Heads and beards were shaved. Their tattered travel clothes were replaced by coarse, damp, grey-striped prison uniforms. Their money and humble personal belongings were confiscated—including the rosaries Abbé Held had given Bud and Bob, a rare source of comfort as they walked through the dark times. Ancient, threadbare blankets were given to each. For protesting the loss of their freedom, they got a punch to the ribs.

They were pointed down a dank, dark, hallway and pushed into a cramped stone cell. Twelve other prisoners were spread around the edges of the dark room, gaunt and listless. Their clothes were ragged and soiled, hair and beards now long and unwashed. There were no beds or other furniture in the cell and no obvious toilet. As his eyes adjusted to the dim light, Bud could see a pipe running down the wall, water trickling into a hole in the floor, and recognized the communal toilet for the cell. The still air stank of death and feces. Bud found it hard to breathe.

Bud and Bob could see an iron-barred single window against the far wall, open to the night air. There was no heat in the room and no light except what came from the hallway and through the window.

"Now I'm a little worried," Bud confided, fighting despair. "This is not what we were hoping for."

"Shades of the Spanish Inquisition," Bob quipped as best he could as his own heart sank. After all they had been through, and their harrowing climb through the mountains, they feared they were about to be sent back to France to face the Nazis, or be forgotten in a Spanish dungeon.

The prison warden, a short, portly Spanish *hombre* with a grizzled beard, his dirty, sweat-stained white shirt straining to cover his belly, came up to the cell and guards opened the door. "Welcome to Castell de Sant Ferran."

"Thank you," replied Bob. Using language suggested by the Army Air Force for evaders, he added, "A pleasure to meet someone who speaks English so well. We are shipwrecked sailors from an Allied plane. How do we get out of here and back to America?"

The man shook his head and spoke without irony.

"You don't."

Bud used more information from his training.

"We just escaped from the Germans. We are not just on the run. We need your help to contact the American government. They will see your help to us as honorable and reward you for your troubles."

Their jailer waved them back into the cell and left without ceremony. A gloom settled over the men. Their new quarters were cold, dark, and forbidding.

Castell de Sant Ferran, on a hill near Figueres in the Catalan region of eastern Spain, had been built as a military fortress in the 18th century, when frequent battles were fought over the border between Spain and France. Its imposing towering thick stone walls were designed to resist cannonballs and repel invaders. At the height of its use, Sant Ferran supported and housed 6,000 troops.

Even in the best of times, there was no comfort for anyone but the highest-level military officers. As it became less needed for military use, San Ferran more recently served as a prison during the Spanish Civil War, one of the worst in Spain. Bud and Bob, Prosser and McLain spent the next three weeks of their lives hoping their stay in this hellhole would be brief.

"Daily life at a prison like this is maybe a step up from a POW camp," Bud offered to his now-cellmate Bob. "It could be worse. I've got a good buddy with me. We're not in a concentration camp. We aren't being grilled by the Jerries. And at least we're in a somewhat neutral country."

Bob's view was bleaker.

"More filthy straw filled with bugs. We have no idea how long we might rot in here. So close to freedom and then it was snatched away. We should have made a run for it. After six months of MIA we're officially deceased! Who's going to come looking for dead guys when there's a war on?"

All too soon they knew the scope of their surroundings. Their cell was closed on three sides and fronted by rough iron bars. They washed themselves in the feeble spurts of water from the rusted wall pipe, the same one that fed the foul latrine just below it. There was no soap or toilet paper. No towels. Their mattress was a sack filled with straw. Thin blankets did little to warm them. Their prison uniforms were quickly filthy. They stayed that way, and the Americans quickly began to resemble their wretched cellmates. The few hours of sunlight visible each day through the high cell window soon faded and again the cell was dark for the interminable hours of night.

The menu was the same every day. Morning brought a cup of dark water posing as coffee and a crust of dry bread. In the afternoon, a watery simulation of soup in wooden bowls with wooden spoons.

Brief opportunities to leave the cell allowed the prisoners to walk around the vast courtyard. Squinting in the Spanish sun, they saw evidence of the brutality of their hosts throughout history. A wall riddled with bullet holes testified to executions that had been commonplace. Looking across the barren yard, Bud knew he was lucky to be alive and hoped to stay that way.

From fellow inmates Bud and Bob learned that the prison held about 300 political prisoners, most of whom had been soldiers fighting against Franco and imprisoned since the late 1930s. These poor souls had no hope of release until he was out of power.

As time went by, the monotony of each day was much greater than it had been in France, the surroundings far worse than anything they had experienced.

"I really miss the cleanliness of our dirt dugout at Château de'Laillé" Bob quipped.

"Living in the dirt outside of a cell looks pretty good to me too!" Bud agreed.

Still, they were out of German-occupied France, a big step closer to home. As always, Bud missed Rosemary. He no longer had the good luck photo of her that he always touched for luck on bombing missions. He felt close to her by daydreaming. He could see himself walking down the aisle with Rosemary on his arm, resplendent in white, while he wore his "Sunday best" dress uniform, standing tall and proud. It would be the start of a balanced, steady life, an American Dream, the opposite of what he was living in the chaos of war where he had little order and less control.

Then again, officially, they were dead.

On Nov. 17, 1943, the day they reached the Spanish border, six months after they went missing in action, the U.S. War Department had officially declared Bud and Bob deceased.

At the same time, their luck had begun to turn. Good things were happening and fast.

Despite their apparent indifference to the flyers' fates, the Spanish authorities did notify the U.S. Consulate of four Americans being held in the prison of Castell de Sant Ferran. The descriptions and ages matched flyers who had been missing in France. Consulate staff couldn't know for sure who they were but nevertheless began to negotiate for their release. An American consul traveled from Madrid, arriving late in the second week of their imprisonment.

At the prison, Bud and Bob were led back upstairs to the reception area, unsure what to expect. Their eyes strained to adjust to the daylight. The jailers gave no sign. Bud's heart was pounding. *Is this when they send us back to the Nazis?* There was no reason to believe otherwise.

Instead, they soon were in the blessed presence of the consul, the first contact with an American official since they had flown out of England. Bud gasped with relief.

"Gentlemen, the American government is proud of you and welcomes you back. Until you are in a secure setting, we won't ask you how you survived. I know that you guys have some stories to tell. Just hang on to them a little longer."

From there it got easier. The consul gave each of the flyers money to buy fruit, cigarettes and bread to supplement the prison diet. The filth was less uncomfortable knowing their release would come.

Nearly a month after their escape from France, on Dec. 15, 1943, the American Embassy arranged for passage to England by way of Gibraltar. The former prisoners were granted five dollars a day for lodging and meals until they were back in England. Now known to have survived the crash, James Wilschke became US Escape and Evader (E&E) 267. Robert Neil became E&E 268.

Arriving in Bristol, England, the men were finally back in Allied territory. They walked across the airfield tarmac and into a Quonset hut full of bustling men wearing American uniforms. The English language flowed like music.

Their re-entry process included verifying that they were the American airmen they claimed to be rather than German spies. Sgt. Samuel Mundenar, a fellow crewman of Bob's from Chelveston, was flown to Bristol to positively identify them face-to-face as his friends and comrades Robert G. Neil and James Wilschke. "I couldn't believe it when I heard it," Mundenar chuckled. "I just had to come to see for myself that it was really you guys. You're a couple of tough buzzards."

Mundenar saluted, then carefully hugged the two "tough" guys.

An officer from MIS-X smiled and sat them at a small table where they were handed paper and pencil. "You guys must have been through a lot. Here, you each get to send a telegram home."

Bud thought for a few minutes. He'd had a thousand conversations with Rosemary in his mind since the crash but not having written anything for months, he struggled to think of the words he wanted to say. Finally, he took a deep breath and started to write. He handed the paper back to the clerk. "Send this, please."

Part Three

At headquarters, they learned that much had changed in the six months they had been away. A lot of new men there, a lot of old friends missing. As Neil said, "the experience was something like going back to the boss after being absent for a long time and saying, Remember me? I used to work here. For the first 20 minutes, you're a visiting celebrity, then you slip back into the old routine."
—Providence Journal interview with Bob Neil, January 1944

Chapter 18

Homecoming

Don't do anything that you would be ashamed to have on the front page of the newspaper.
—Bud Wilschke

Rosemary Crandell stepped off the streetcar in the late afternoon and quickly walked along Woodlawn Avenue towards home, the sharp, December wind nipping at her legs and ankles. One hand clutched her scarf to her neck, and the other held her hat tightly to prevent it from sailing off in a blustery blast. Head bent down, she just wanted to get home after a busy day at the real estate office. She was glad that she usually didn't have much time to think about anything else at work, but as she rode the streetcar home, she began her daily reflection on the war and her family. The latest news from George was that he was safe aboard his ship, the USS Dale. It was in the South Pacific, escorting a damaged ship back to San Francisco, so that was a relief from worry. But more than six months had passed since Bud was declared MIA back in May, and now with no word from him or notice that he was captured and a POW, the government considered him officially KIA. She couldn't bear to think of it. Rosemary simply had to believe that somewhere, Bud was alive and would come back to her.

Climbing the steps to her front door and stepping inside, she was alarmed to see her mom and dad waiting for her with anxious faces. Her dad held a yellow envelope. Western Union, addressed to her.

"We knew you would be home soon, dear, so we waited for you," her mother said with deep concern in her eyes.

Rosemary didn't say anything as she carefully unpinned her hat and lay it on the hall table. She took a deep breath, and with trembling hands, gently took the envelope from her father. Rosemary turned away, carefully slit the telegram open, and read the brief message while her parents looked on, hoping the news was not bad.

Then, with a shriek of joy Rosemary spun around and grabbed her dad in a hug, then her mother. Harry took the message and read it out loud.

WRITE ME AT MY OLD APO AND SET THE WEDDING FOR FEBRUARY—JIM.

"My prayers have been answered!" Rosemary cried, tears beginning to stream down her face. The telegram back in her still-trembling hands, she could barely believe how her life had changed in an instant. Of the many wonderful days in her life the best may have been this day, the day she received news from her beloved Bud. He was alive! And coming home to be a part of her life again.

Mabel was thrilled and excited for her daughter too. She knew this meant they had to get busy—there was a lot to prepare now that a wedding was just two months off. But Christmas that year would now be a joyful one, and even busier than usual.

The news somehow made it quickly to the newspapers across Chicago, and they trumpeted the news that Bud, a local MIA airman, had survived and was safe. People couldn't get enough of this feel-good story of triumph in the winter of 1943-44, when the outcome of the war wasn't at all a sure thing.

A sampling of the inspiring headlines cheered and celebrated by Chicagoans:

PROPOSAL IS 1st WORD OF FLYER LOST 7 MONTHS
(12/28/43)

At least one girl in Chicago knows that dreams come true. She is Miss Rosemary Crandell, 21, a secretary, who never lost faith that she would one day hear from her fiancé, Lt. James S. Wilschke, 23, a bombardier reported missing in action over Europe last June. Through seven months she hoped and waited, but there was no word. Now she is making wedding plans!

THEIR SIGHTS ARE TRAINED ON HAPPINESS
(1/8/44 *Chicago Daily News*)

Lt. James S. Wilschke, bombardier, reported missing in action over Europe for seven months, was back home today happily reunited with his fiancée, Rosemary Crandell.

MISSING FLYER SAFE, TUNES UP WEDDING BELLS

Miss Rosemary Crandell, 21, of 8034 Woodlawn Ave, had joyful news today. It was contained in a cablegram which said "Write or cable me at my old APO and plan for wedding in February. Jim"

Behind that message lay seven months of heartbreaking suspense, during which time, her Lieutenant had been listed officially as missing.

A WAR STORY; A LOVE STORY; A GOOD STORY!
(1/4/44 *Daily News*)

Rosemary Crandell's seven-month vigil of hope and faith that her fiancé, Lt. James S. Wilschke, 23, a bombardier who has been reported missing over Europe since May 17, would come back has been rewarded.

Bud's mom, Mrs. Mabel Wilschke, was also interviewed. "It was the first word we had received from him in more than seven months, but I never gave up hope. I placed him in God's hands and I know that the prayers of all his friends have brought him back."

ROSEMARY CRANDELL WINKS AT FATE

After long months of heartbreaking silence, Lt. James S. Wilschke was today not only back from the land of the missing after seven months, but is planning to be married to fiancée Rosemary Crandell, 21, his high school sweetheart.

ADVENTURE BEHIND, ROMANCE AHEAD,
FLYER BAILS OUT HERE—ALTAR BOUND

Missing flyer returns to the arms of his fiancée. There was many a time since he had to bail out over enemy-held European territory that Lt. James S. Wilschke thought he was never going to get a girl in his arms. Then he bailed out eagerly from the Manhattan Limited in Chicago and THE girl was in his arms.

FLYER'S WAR STORY IS SECRET,
BUT HIS WEDDING PLANS AREN'T

Though how he managed it is shrouded in secrecy, Lt. James S. Wilschke, 23, a bombardier reported MIA over occupied Europe for seven months, successfully returned home today.

AIR HERO RETURNS TO GET HIS GIRL
(1/17/44, *The Chicago Sun*)

Lt. James Wilschke, 23-year-old bombardier, had to bail out over enemy territory in Europe last May and was missing for seven months before working his way through enemy lines back to Britain and now to a happy-ending wedding in Chicago.

The wedding was quickly organized and the joyful ceremony held on Jan. 15, 1944. Rosemary initially argued with the priest at St. Francis de Paula Church about whether or not the "to obey" wedding vow needed to be included. The priest, a traditionalist, told her she was fortunate to have her man back from the war and therefore should be happy to do what he asked. She acquiesced, knowing she could trust Bud no matter what the vows said.

To save money, they borrowed dresses from another girl's recent wedding party. Like he had imagined as a forlorn prisoner in Spain, Rosemary was luminous in her white dress and train and Bud looked dashing in his dress uniform, although it was slightly too big for him after his ordeal. The elegant afternoon reception was held in a local hotel, serving finger sandwiches, punch, tea and a layered cake with white frosting. Years later, Rosemary told her daughter Sue that after the ceremony, the couple was still so wound

Rosemary, Bud, and wedding party 1944.

Rosemary and Bud in Chicago 1944.

up that they went to a movie to calm down before setting off on their brief honeymoon.

Two weeks after the wedding, Bud was sent to Los Angeles, California. Three weeks later he was assigned to Midland Army Airfield in Midland, Texas for the rest of the war. At Midland, he spent his tour training new bombardier recruits. In July 1945, he was transferred to another base near Chicago and was discharged in October of that year.

After the war, Bud went to work as a linesman for Illinois Bell Telephone Co. in Chicago. He enlisted in the Illinois Army National Guard, retiring after 20 years at the rank of Captain.

Bud and Rosemary's first child, a girl, was born on Christmas Day in 1944. They named her Jeanne in honor of Bud's helper, Jeanne Sébastien, of Nantes, and after the beach house they were first sheltered in at Saint-Pierre-Quiberon. The family grew to two boys and three girls, all helping breed and train champion Springer Spaniel dogs in Clarendon Hills, a Chicago suburb.

Bud was issued a new flight jacket. It was a badge of honor even though he would no longer fly in the B-17. Still. he continued to think about his first one and how it had protected him in the plane and during his only parachute jump. He wished he'd been able to keep it, but he had survived.

*   *   *   *

September 10, 1944
Dear Jim,
I've been going to do this for quite some time but didn't get around to it. You know how it is!!

Hoppy heard you were still kicking through his wife. Kinda expected to hear from you but guess you've lost track of me. Was glad to hear that you were married. Of course I expected it so it wasn't a surprise. Hope you are getting along okay. Give Rosemary my love and tell her to get the house ready for our reunion. What a party that will be. Wolfe, Hoppy, Toyek, Wolinski and I all live together. They send their regards and hope to see you soon. Have you seen A. P. lately?

*Suppose he's happy to settle down again after his travels. I've
written several cards to Lallah but haven't heard from her
yet. Well Jim—Be Good and we'll all see you soon—Always
a Pal—Ken*

Handwritten letter from Ken Kenyon, from POW camp
Stalag VIIA

Over the years, Bud received letters from many of his war mates and
fellow soldiers. Sometimes he would leave the envelopes unopened
for a week or more. Rosemary would often help him write a reply,
thanking his friends for their support and friendship. She would fill
in details about the family's life and stories about their children. At
other times, she helped him deal with the military, including a challenge to the definition of who was a prisoner of war.

Rosemary sat down in their den one morning, rolled a fresh
sheet of paper into her typewriter and waited for his dictation. Bud
didn't relish stepping back into his old story again, but knew he
might be able to help many other current and past servicemen get
the benefits that they had earned.

"Where should we start? They are asking for details about your
separation from your Unit, how you escaped the enemy and the
circumstances of your return to Allied control."

Bud began retelling his story about his experiences in France
and Spain.

"My report made to Military Intelligence at the time of repa-
triation completely omitted my internment in Spain, as required.
Because of the sensitive nature of wartime events in a neutral country, the facts are secret even today."

"That's a good opening," Rosemary encouraged. "Now let's tell
them the story you had to leave out in that first report."

Now Bud was able to provide the missing chapter.

"It was arranged for us to leave France at night early in November.
Our host took us by car to a location outside of Perpignan, France,
where we were met by a guide and more than a dozen other men
anxious to cross the border.

"Crossing the border two days later, we were arrested by Spanish police and transferred to the federal prison in Gerona. We were interrogated multiple times, but only gave our name, rank and serial number and requested to see the American consul. We were held in a prison and deprived of the rights of military prisoners according to the Geneva Convention. We had no reason to believe we would ever be released."

"A concise summary," said Rosemary. "Now let's see what the results may be. Bud, I'm sure your letter will make a difference for MIAs as well as Escapees and Evaders to get the benefits and recognition of service that they are due."

In 1990, Bud and Bob learned that the Veterans Administration had amended the definition of Prisoner of War to include former service members detained in the line of duty during wartime by allied or neutral governments, not only applicable to those who had been held in an enemy POW camp. This included their stay in a Spanish prison.

Chapter 19

Bob Neil Returns to Providence

Bob Neil's most pleasant experience since being home? . . . The ride home from New York to Providence on the train. It was so carefree and comfortable. You just know the conductor won't yell, "Bail out!"
—Providence Journal interview with Bob Neil, January 1944.

It seemed to Bob that the entire city had turned out to see the annual Christmas parade. He was invited to join as way for the townspeople to express their joy and relief that one of their hometown boys had returned safely. Bob and his friend Eddie Fontaine, another escapee he met in the prison in Castell de Sant Ferran, were honorees, even though Bob didn't feel like he was a hero at all. How was it that he was the one who survived the awful explosion and crash? Bob couldn't get over the feelings of guilt that somehow he had survived when the others hadn't made it.

Bob Neil 1944.

The parade route snaked through town to the Roger Williams Park bandstand, where a few town elders would make speeches about how brave and honorable the men were. A photographer from the *Providence Journal* was there to document the parade and took some shots of the hometown heroes in the back of an open convertible. They moved slowly down the street, the high school band marching ahead of the open cars and floats gaily decorated with Christmas lights. As the band drew near, excitement mounted. They played "Stars and Stripes Forever," "America the Beautiful," Christmas carols and the high school pep song. People cheered and waved at the band and dignitaries.

Although he was cheered by the crowds, Bob felt lonely. He wanted a girlfriend. Leaning into his buddy's shoulder, he said, "Eddie, let's go to the Rhodes-on-the-Pawtuxet tomorrow night. Jimmy Dorsey has a show at nine that should be terrific. It'll be lousy with sailors but the girls will see how much better dancers we airmen are."

Ed laughed and gently elbowed Bob as he waved at the crowd and the men settled in for the cold ride. Eddie had been shot down over France on September 15 and made it to Spain in 45 days. His fiancée, Rita Grenier, had been waiting for him to come home and they had just announced their wedding plans in the papers. He asked Bob to be their best man.

Bob and Ed's photo ran on the front page of the *Journal* the next morning along with their stories of being shot down over France. They were the talk of the town that day.

That evening, June Claire Davis took the trolley from her home in Pawtucket to work at her cashier's job at the Rhodes nightclub, expecting nothing but the typical routine of customers and chores. June was a young pretty brunette with brown eyes and a quick smile. She'd worked as cashier at the Rhodes-on-the-Pawtuxet for a couple of years, but was lonely like almost all the girls she knew. She didn't have a special fella or anyone to even write to. She had spent too many nights dealing with rowdy sailors but knew there would be the right man for her someday. She hoped the war would end so all the young men would come home.

June took her place at the checkout counter and glanced at the folded newspaper lying next to the cash register. As she looked at the photo of Bob and Ed, she was especially taken with Technical Sergeant Robert Neil, so handsome in his uniform, smiling and waving. Her pal at work, Libby, stood next to her, giggling and poring over the story and the picture of the handsome men. Impulsively, June confidently tapped the photo with her finger and said, "I'm going to marry that man!"

That evening as Bob came into the Rhodes with his friend, he saw the dance floor full of girls, some dancing with sailors and some partnered with other girls. He felt a little self-conscious in his new uniform. He glanced down again and felt to make sure his tie was straight.

Bob's mind flashed to the little farm in France where he hid only eight months earlier. It was the last place he saw the uniform he had worn flying out of Chelveston, England to bomb Lorient, France. Pangs of worry engulfed him as he began to sweat a bit. It seemed like a world away, and it was, but those farmers who helped him were still there under occupation. Were they still alive? Would they survive the war?

He returned to the moment. He and Ed started to make their way through the smoky room to the bar.

"What'll you have, Bob?"

"How about a cognac?"

It was Bob's little joke. He turned, leaned back on his elbows and scanned the room.

"Eddie, I'm going to marry the first girl I dance with!"

June and Libby saw a commotion at the door as two uniformed men entered. The girls shared a sidelong look and big smiles when they saw it was the two guys in the photo. As the flyers walked by, June was ready, and it was easy to flirt with Bob as their eyes met.

"Excuse me, Libby, I have to go powder my nose," she winked, and turned to head Bob's way.

As June passed by, Bob said loudly over the music, "Great band! Would you like to dance?"

As they squeezed onto the dance floor, it was the best feeling of Bob's life. It was easy for them to fall in love.

Bob and June had a whirlwind romance and married on March 11, 1944.

Unfortunately, Bob's trauma and survivor's guilt (now understood as Post Traumatic Stress Disorder or PTSD) took a toll on his mental health and the marriage. Bob and June had four children before they divorced. Bob did not remarry.

A career salesman, as his children grew, he loved to talk about current events, geography, and history. Like many of his generation he did not reveal his emotions, though they believe they could see the sadness in his eyes.

Bob stayed involved with his Catholic faith, read the Bible regularly and tried all his life to come to terms with the tragedies of his youth. He died September 27, 1992, at age 70.

Chapter 20

Reunion

Food was in very short supply as most food was rationed and our helpers had to share their meager supply with us. Also when we were being hidden in the woods, abandoned houses, churches, etc., it was very difficult to bring us food on a regular basis. As a result of this, plus the amount of walking that we did, I lost about 40 pounds in the seven months that I was missing.

All of the evaders would have had similar harrowing experiences.

The flyers who had been wounded could only be given minimal care by their helpers and if the wounds were too severe for medical care available, they were deposited near a German installation for capture and treatment.
—Bud Wilschke personal statement challenging the
Former POW Benefits Act of 1981

Returning to America, Bud soon regained the 40 pounds lost during his hikes across France. A sturdy man to begin with, his physical education and coaching background helped him build his physical strength once again.

The emotional wounds from the time in France were harder to heal, but Rosemary was the emotional rock he could depend on. She steadied the course of his life over the ensuing years. When she saw that Bud was stressed by people's expectations or his own memories, she was at his side.

One autumn morning in 1982, Bud sat at his kitchen table in the family's Mount Dora, Florida, home, his hand wrapped around a cold cup of coffee. Rosemary had just returned with groceries for the dinner Bud would grill that night. As she put the milk in the refrigerator, their daughter Sue stopped over to see how her parents were doing. She hugged her mom and sat down.

"You look tired, Dad."

Rosemary was concerned. She had noticed his restless sleep the night before.

"It was one of those nights again," he said. "I'm tired today. A lot of memories come back to me.

"Anything you want to tell us about?"

Nothing new, it just keeps happening. Sometimes when I try to sleep, I can hear that plane coming apart in the air. And then, I think, what if Indiere had made a different decision? What if he turned around and went back to base? Just dump those bombs in the Channel and go back out the next mission with all four engines working and do the job right. Roy, Cullinan, Mitchell, Schenk, the rest of them, we all would've gotten another chance and those guys might've survived. Why did I get to come back and have the life I have?"

Rosemary stood behind him, rubbing his shoulders. "I know you would've done anything to save those guys. It just wasn't your call, darling."

Bud's dog moved up against his leg and Bud rubbed his ears.

"Bud, next May it will be 40 years," Rosemary counseled. "I wonder if it isn't time to go back to visit France again, see those places and the people who cared for you, and made it possible for you to survive."

He laughed. "Can we go by boat?"

While he felt dread about flying after his World War II experiences, Bud would not have missed this reunion and didn't take long to agree to do whatever it took.

"No, I think you're right," he said. "We could go back now. I've been remembering the war and it's been getting me stirred up. But I think about those wonderful people, too. Yes, I believe you're right, let's do it."

Quickly organizing the epic return trip, Rosemary wrote to Antoine Dreano, who as a teenager had brought meals to Bud and Bob when they were hiding at the Chapelle Sainte-Brigitte à Landévant and practiced his English with them. Dreano was now a physician with his own family.

Rosemary booked tickets and made arrangements with Dr. Dreano who eagerly hosted Bud and Rosemary at his home in

Antoine Dreano and Rosemary 1983.   *Marion Wilke ("Roger the Mute")*
                                          and Bud 1983.

Trelecan. Dreano organized meaningful visits as he accompanied Bud and Rosemary around Brittany.

The Wilschkes were honored guests at numerous commemorative ceremonies at which they met up with several of Bud's old friends. They had tearful reunions with Félix Jouan's daughter, Annick, and with Marian Wilke— "Roger the Mute." They visited several of Bud's hiding places, including the Château de Laillé where a permanent stone altar had been erected at the site of the secret 1943 Mass.

Wherever they went, small crowds of friends and family of their helpers gathered to offer gratitude for Bud's service to them. They

Villa Jeanne, Quiberon, France.

posed for pictures and served *Breton* cake and traditional hard cider. Then on to the next site. All along the way, Bud marveled that the beauty of the countryside and the graciousness of his hosts hadn't changed.

Dreano drove them in his Citroën up the lanes to Ploemel. At the small rural village where Bud had landed after bailing out 40 years earlier, the visitors were joined by the mayor and other citizens on a sunny morning at the local cemetery, where Bud wanted to pay his respects to Mathurin Diabat, the farmer in whose pasture Bud had first landed.

The crowd grew and Bud was surprised at the number of people smiling and nodding at him. A local reporter was taking notes. As they stood on a gravel path among the gravestones, Bud gripped Rosemary's hand as he recalled Diabat's heroism and how he risked his and his family's lives to save him.

After a short prayer of thanks, Bud turned to Dreano.

Diabat cemetery plot.

"I wonder if André Diabat still lives in the area?"

André, son of Mathurin Diabat, was about Bud's age and had helped Bud hide at the Diabat farm.

The Diabat loft.

Mathurin Diabat.

Bud and André Diabat 1983.

Alice Diabat 2017.

After a momentary rustle in the crowd, a weathered man in a flat cap stepped forward, his face easily familiar to Bud despite the years.

"I am here!"

He called out, smiling, a twinkle in his eye, pleased that Bud had remembered him. He put his arm around the petite woman next to him.

"Here is my sister too! Remember little Alice?"

Eager to share his joy and excitement at Bud's return, André Diabat invited Bud and Rosemary and the whole crowd to visit the family farm.

Emotions and memories flowed through Bud as they drove along the green fields and hedgerows toward the Diabat farm. Suddenly, there it was, the old stone farmhouse, added to over the years, surrounded by small stone out-buildings. He inhaled the aromas of the farm and fields, rich and fragrant. An old wooden ladder leaned against the barn wall, leading up to the loft where he had spent his first night in France.

Not far away was the field where he had crashed into the fence and come face-to-face with Mathurin Diabat's shotgun. Farther on, he saw the hedgerow where he had hidden while the Germans searched for him.

Joy and sadness swelled in him, and Bud fell to his knees in front of the farmhouse and kissed the ground. Rosemary and his French hosts stood by, ready to comfort him. The crowd stood in a semi-circle around him, watching with affection and respect. All felt the importance of the moment. Taking a deep breath, Bud gathered himself and stood. He tried to say a few words of thanks to the crowd.

André reached out and put his hand on Bud's shoulder.

"James, please wait here a moment."

Bud with his jacket 1983.

He walked quickly toward the front of the house and stepped inside. Bud stood with Rosemary, not sure what would happen next. A minute or two later, André came out with his arms wrapped around an astonishing gift.

"M. Wilschke, my family was honored to protect you. My father spoke of you often until his final breath. He had a premonition that he would see you again, but when he died it became my privilege to keep this for you. We kept it safe in my closet for your return."

André bowed as he proudly presented a familiar bundle of shearling leather, Bud's original flying jacket, as if it were the medal of the *Légion d'honneur*. There was an audible gasp and then applause from the crowd.

Bud leaned against the side of the farmhouse, gripping the jacket. He buried his face in his arm and wept as he absorbed the memories and honor of the moment. For five minutes, he cried as he remembered himself and Bob Neil as two scared American boys who somehow managed to survive.

After retiring to Florida, Bud and Rosemary hosted a French exchange student as an opportunity to give back to and honor the French people who had helped him. Cendrine Rodrigues, now a Canadian citizen, remained in contact with the Wilschke family. She has been wonderfully helpful in researching this project, guiding the contacts with French historians and translating documents.

James S. Wilschke, "Bud," died peacefully October 1, 2001, in Pompano Beach, Florida, at age 81. His obituary said that, a Lieutenant, he had served three years as a bombardier in the 305th Airborne Division. His plane had been shot down over France in 1943 and he was missing in action for seven months while he made his way back to the Allied lines via the French Underground. He was awarded several medals, including the Purple Heart.

Chapter 21

Epilogue

We will never forget.
—Motto of Air Forces Escape and Evasion Society

On October 13, 2001, just over a month after the September 11 terrorist attacks on New York and Washington, D.C., a group of French and American citizens gathered at a roadside park near the village of Brec'h, Brittany, France.

They came to dedicate a *stele*, or memorial, to honor the ten aviators of B-17F Flying Fortress #42-5219 that crashed at that site over 58 years earlier. The group included Pierre Sauvet, 81, the teacher who had met James "Bud" Wilschke just after his World War II crash landing so many years before.

The stele in Brec'h, Brittany, France.

The village had built a large stone monument and plaque listing all ten crew members of B-17 42-5219. It was located not far from where Sauvet had first discovered Lt. James Wilschke when he parachuted into the Diabat farm on May 17, 1943.

Our Bud Wilschke had been invited but had been forced to decline due to poor health. Copilot Joe Boyle, who in 1943 had been captured nearby and imprisoned as a POW, was the only original survivor able to travel and attend the ceremony.

Boyle later described the scene:

The crew of B17 43 5219.

*In a roadside park in the village of Brec'h near Vannes
on the south coast of Brittany a few hundred yards from
where our plane came down, a monument was dedicated to
the memory of our crew. There were bagpipes, a color guard,
a three-star General (ret'd.) from the French Air Force, the
Mayor of Brec'h, an American officer from the American
Cemetery in Normandy, a member of the French House of
Deputies for Brittany, a member of the French National Red
Cross, the President of the "Souvenir de France," and over a
hundred local farmers and townsfolk, many of whom had
witnessed this episode of the air war 58 years ago. There
were two very moving speeches thanking us profusely for the
sacrifices America made in restoring freedom to France and
sympathizing with us for the tragedy of September 11. Both
national anthems were played.*

M. Sauvet had been happy to learn from Boyle that he believed
Bud was alive. Caught up in the emotions of the ceremony and his
memories of their relationship, he was moved to write to his old
friend. Several weeks later, Rosemary received Sauvet's handwritten
letter from France in which he recounted what he saw that day the
men met, and how he helped Bud hide from the German soldiers.

Auray October 17th
SAUVET Pierre
19 Rue du DREZEN
56400 Auray, France

Sir
*You will probably be very surprised on getting my letter. I
have just got your address.*
*I saw you only once and 58 years ago. I was at the time
a teacher in a small village, in Ploërmel, France southern
Brittany.*
*On that day, May 17th, 1943 I suddenly saw a low fly-
ing plane with German fighters behind. We heard the rattle
of machine guns. Then I saw three men bale out and drop.*

Two of them fell near the railway line. The train coming from Quiberon was just passing there. The Germans in the train pulled the communications cord, the train stopped and both men were taken prisoners.

The other man dropped near a small hamlet, a few hundred yards away. A friend of mine and I rushed to the place. When we got there the German motorcyclists from the village were speeding along the road nearby. The farmer took us to the place where he had hidden you under a heap of clover in a shed at the back of the farm house.

I spoke to you, because I knew English. You showed me your identity card and since then, I have never forgotten your name and your address at the time. (1017 Ridgeland Ave. Chicago).

I told you, you could not stay there because the Germans would certainly come and the farmer would be shot and you taken prisoner. You agreed to be hidden elsewhere but you could not walk because your leg was sore. So we helped you. We first wanted to hide you in a rye field on the slope of the hill. But we thought it was dangerous and we hid you in a corner of a thick hedgerow among high ferns. I told you to remain there until the farmer came and fetched you and I went back to the school.

The Germans came a few moments later, climbed into an apple tree and looked at the field. They also bayonetted the heap of clover but they did not find you and I have never seen you again.

As you are as old as I (we were both born in 1921), I was very glad when I heard you were still living. We shall never see each other but I wanted to tell you how grateful I am to you, your comrades in arms and to the American Nation. Until my dying day I will never forget it.

I hope we are both going to live for a long time.

May God bless you and your family

Yours sincerely,

Pierre Sauvet

No one at the ceremony knew that Bud had passed away just days earlier.

Crew

Ten men crewed B17 42-5219 on its final flight. The six who died in the crash were first buried at the civilian cemetery in Vannes, France.

Pilot—2nd Lt. Harry Warren Indiere
POW

Lt. Harry Indiere

Lt. Harry Indiere was born January 12, 1919, and raised in Huntington Station, Long Island, New York, about 40 miles east of New York City. His parents, Pasquale (Patsy) and Angelina Indiere, were both born in Italy, according to the 1930 federal census. Harry's father, Pasquale, had died on May 27, 1941, at age 74. His mother, Angelina, died in 1952 at 62. Youngest of eight, he had three brothers and four sisters. He played basketball at Huntington high school and studied engineering at the University of Cincinnati.

Harry enlisted 19 days after Pearl Harbor on December 26, 1941, at Mitchel Field, Hempstead, New York. In flight school, he became pals with Joe Boyle. After training, they were assigned to different crews.

Indiere flew as co-pilot on 15 missions before May 17, 1943. On this raid, his 16th, he was in the captain's seat for the first time. It was his first and only mission with Joe Boyle.

After the crash, Boyle was reunited with Indiere ("his close friend") at the Vannes train station. Indiere was limping badly. His chute had become tangled in a tree. The Germans cut him free. When he dropped to the ground, he injured his leg so badly that he could barely walk. Escorted by German guards, Harry and Joe were only able to say a few words before climbing aboard the train.

On arrival in Paris, the Germans took Indiere to the American Hospital in Paris for treatment of his injury. According to Boyle's oral history in "A Wartime Log," by Art Beltrone, he reunited with Indiere at Stalag Luft III, where they spent almost two full years as roommates before liberation in April 1945. To pass the long hours, they fashioned golf clubs and putters from wood trim scrounged from the barracks. Using his engineering skills, Indiere fashioned golf balls from wax, old boot leather, and small pieces of old basketballs. They were designed to not fly too far so they wouldn't lose them over the fence. An old milk can sufficed for the hole. They played for Canadian candy bars. A hole-in-one was worth half a candy bar.

After the war, Indiere returned to Suffolk County on Long Island. He died in 1993 at the age of 74 and is buried at St. Patrick's Cemetery in Huntington Station, Long Island.

Co-Pilot—Lt. Joseph Baxter Boyle
POW

Lt. Joseph Boyle was born August 25, 1918, in Yukon Territory, Canada, and grew up in Teaneck, New Jersey. He earned a BA in business administration from Lehigh University in 1939. In 1942, he joined the Army Air Force, trained as a pilot and was assigned to the B-17 *Dry Martini and the Cocktail Kids*, piloted by Captain Allen Martini. Boyle had flown 14 missions over France and Germany as a co-pilot, hoping to move up to the pilot's seat one day.

Joe Boyle

According to Boyle's oral history in *War Eagles*, by Michael Norwood McDowell: "I was part of a pick-up crew of relative strangers and following the briefing that morning, we loaded up the airplane . . . it was still before dawn . . . we were flying with Harry Indiere, and in the tail we had Sgt. Mitchell . . . those two were the only ones I had seen before . . . it was truly a pick-up crew."

May 17, 1943, was Boyle's 15th mission.

Boyle passed out briefly after a hard landing in a cabbage field, his parachute snagged above him in a tree. He was trying to get his cumbersome flying boots off when a group of regular German soldiers approached. One of the soldiers spoke English and cheerfully told Boyle that for him, the war was over. As they stood around him a young German SS officer, scarred face and all, came roaring up on a motorcycle, pulled out his Luger and ended the chitchat. He ordered Boyle to get in the sidecar and they drove off. Not far away, the SS officer and Boyle pulled up about 50 yards from a smoldering crashed B-17. As he had barely seen the outside of the plane before taking off in the early morning, Boyle couldn't tell if it was the same plane he'd flown earlier that day.

The SS officer took him to a former dental office that had been requisitioned by the Nazis and showed him jewelry that had been taken from the bodies of flyers in the aircraft. Boyle recognized a watch that belonged to Henry Mitchell. After spending a night in a local jail, Boyle was taken to the Vannes railroad station (about 25 miles west of Brec'h) to be transported to Paris. He was soon incarcerated with Indiere in Poland at Stalag Luft III (of *The Great Escape* fame).

Boyle and Indiere were aware of the ongoing escape activities in the camp and assumed roles as "penguins," shuffling throughout the camp and scattering sand dug from the tunnels. They devised narrow sacks inside their trousers to release sand with a pull of a string that was threaded up into their pockets. Of the Brits who escaped and were later captured and executed by the Germans, Boyle said, "We knew all of them; we felt terrible."

Boyle was a talented artist and spent hours sketching, drawing cartoons and writing poetry. Other prisoners asked him to sketch portraits for them. Later, his drawings and poems were published in various books, articles and publications, including *A Wartime Log*, by Art and Lee Beltrone (1995) and *Clipped Wings*, by O. M. Chiesl, (1948).

As the Allied troops closed in, the POWs were forced to participate in "The Long March," and ultimately were freed by General George Patton's troops in April 1945. By then, Boyle had lost 40 pounds. Back home, he was awarded the Distinguished Flying Cross and a Purple Heart.

After the war, Boyle returned to New Jersey and married Nancy

Cavanaugh and had three children. He owned a carpet and furniture business before retiring and enjoying golf and his grandchildren. His daughter Leslie Shipps, recalls him saying about the war, "I am burdened by total recall."

In 2001, Boyle was invited to participate in the dedication of the memorial erected by the citizens of Brec'h to honor the ten men aboard 42-5219. He died on his 91st birthday, in 2009.

SUCH SCANTY FARE
By Joseph Boyle

The fate we share as prisoners,
Is drab and often grim,
Existing on such scanty fare,
As Reich-bread, spuds and klim.
Beds and books and little else,
To fill Time's flapping sail,
She makes or loses headway all,
Depending on the mail.
Oh! Drab the days and slow to pass,
With this barbed-wire fence,
When all the joys of living are
Still in the future tense.
So here's to happy days ahead
When you and I are free
To look back on this interlude
And call it history

(Klim was milk powder—milk spelled backwards)

Navigator—2nd Lt. Roy Eugene Richards
KIA

Lt. Roy Richards was born August 4, 1918, in Red Lake Falls, a small farming town in northwestern Minnesota, about 45 miles east of Grand Forks, North Dakota. He was one of seven children of Edward, a farmer, and Mary Ann (Dougherty) Richards, who died in 1921.

Roy Richards

Roy met and married Audrey Squier from Des Moines, Iowa, where he enlisted in the Army Air Forces. Beginning April 17, 1943, he flew six missions over Belgium, Germany and France.

Bud Wilschke saved two newspaper clippings about Richards' memorial service and his widow. There is also a letter in Bob Neil's papers from Audrey's father, dated August 9, 1944, asking Neil for any details he might be able to share about Richards' death.

Roy Richards is buried at the Normandy American Cemetery at Colleville-sur-Mer, France.

Flight Engineer/Top Turret T/Sgt. John W. McFarland
KIA

John McFarland

Sgt. "Johnny" McFarland was born in 1919 near Houghton in Michigan's Upper Peninsula. He dropped out of school at age 15 to find a job and help support the family. He and his mother, Victoria, moved to Chicago, where he walked her to St. Boniface Catholic Church every morning when his schedule allowed. He met Ellen Deffenbaugh through a sales job. They married September 15, 1941. Johnny signed up for the Army Air Force five months later, on February 26, 1942.

May 17th was McFarland's eighth mission as Engineer/TTG.

After McFarland was killed, Ellen did not remarry. She traveled to France in later years to find out more about her husband's death. She remained close to the McFarland family until she passed away at age 95. John is buried at the Normandy American Cemetery at Colleville-sur-Mer, France.

Ball Turret gunner SSgt. Walter Edgar Schenk
KIA

Sgt. Walter "Buddy" Schenk was born June 19, 1919, and raised in Mt. Vernon, Indiana, a small town on the Ohio River. He had two brothers and three sisters. As a baby, he was given over to the care of his Aunt Tina and her husband, Fred Schenk, who joyfully raised him as their only child. Schenk's mother, Beatrice, married C. Cecil Gibson after her first husband (and Walter's father) was murdered during the dark days of Prohibition.

Walter Schenk

Walter's younger sister, Ruth, remembers how as a teenager, "Buddy" would swim the width of the Ohio River over to Kentucky, just for fun. He graduated from St. Matthew's Catholic High School and worked about a year before enlisting in the Army Air Force. First assigned to the 347th Service Squadron, 328th Service Group, Schenk's letters back home to Ruth and the family always said he was fine, there wasn't much news to tell, and that he could not disclose his actual location. He loved the hand-knitted socks Ruth sent and told her how much her work at home to support the war effort was appreciated.

Schenk transferred to the 364th BS of the 305th in the spring of 1943. Beginning on April 16, he flew five successful missions with the *Spitz Fire* crew of Lt. Frank R. Spitznagel, Jr, until he was assigned to the fated pickup crew of Indiere's plane on May 17, 1943. A short description by Bob Neil in his E&E report indicated that Schenk was hit and wounded badly, with face and hand burns, and no oxygen on at 27,000 feet when the bail-out bell sounded. His family chose to have his remains returned home for burial at the St. Matthew's Cemetery in Mt. Vernon.

John Norris

Left Waist Gunner Sgt. John D. Norris
KIA

Sgt. John Norris was born October 13, 1920, third of six children, four boys and two girls. His parents, George and Florence, emigrated from England in 1915 and settled in Turtle Creek, Pennsylvania, a suburb of Pittsburgh. He had several nicknames growing up: Jack, Jackie, and Spratt— "Jack Spratt." After he graduated from Turtle Creek high school, he got a job at the Westinghouse plant in town. When war broke out, Norris wanted to fly airplanes but with his limited vision, he worked as an aircraft mechanic. He was sent to England and assigned to the 364th as a gunner on April 14, 1943. He flew five missions with the 364th, beginning May 4th. He kept this news from his family. His parents first learned he was a B-17 gunner when the MIA telegram arrived on May 17. His family had his remains returned to the U.S. He is buried in the military section at Church Hill Cemetery in Turtle Creek.

Right Waist Gunner SSgt. Dennis Timothy Cullinan, Jr.
KIA

Dennis Cullinan

Sgt. Dennis Cullinan was born November 5, 1919, in Bangor, Maine, to Dennis and Mary McCarthy Cullinan. His mother died when he was about three, after the birth of his sister. Cullinan was the seventh Dennis Timothy in their family, stretching back to 1638.

Dennis enlisted in the Army Air Corps in 1938, (this became the Army Air Force in 1941, and the Air Force in 1947) and trained at Shepard Field in Kansas and the Las Vegas Gunnery School. He was assigned to the 19th Bombardment Group in the Pacific and wounded in action at the Battle of the Coral Sea, May 1942, the first setback for the Japanese forces. After his recovery, Cullinan was reassigned to the 8th Air Force in Europe, first to the 366th BS then the 364th BS of the 305th Bomb Group and flew two missions before the May 17 mission. He is buried at the Normandy American Cemetery at Colleville-sur-Mer, France.

Tail Gunner—SSgt. Henry Aaron Mitchell, Jr.
KIA

Sgt. Henry Mitchell was born December 4, 1917 (Some sources say 1919), to Henry and Eufrosina Mitchell in Pampanga, Philippines, where his dad, Henry Mitchell Sr. was a First Sergeant at Clark Air Force Base. It was reported that Henry Sr. served on the staff of General MacArthur.

Henry Jr. married a Filipino woman and they had one child. In the early 1940s, he was employed as a shipmate in the engine room on the U.S. merchant ship *American Manufacturer*, sailing between New York City and the Philippines. He enlisted in the U.S. Army Air Force from New York City with the Seaman's House YMCA listed as his address.

Henry Mitchell, Jr.

Mitchell was assigned as tail gunner to the crew of pilot Allen Martini's plane *Dry Martini and the Cocktail Kids*. One of his raids was written up in a 1944 *Saturday Evening Post* story, "*15 Minutes over Paris*." He flew 18 missions before being shot down May 17, his body found in the fuselage of the crashed plane.

Mitchell received the Distinguished Flying Cross citation and Purple Heart. After the war, his family had his remains buried at the American Cemetery in Manila, Philippines. Mitchell's wife and child did not survive the Japanese invasion of the Philippines. Many members of the extended family immigrated to the United States and live in the Long Beach, California, area.

B-17F Flying Fortress #42-5219

Manned by a crew of ten, the many heavy machine guns that bristled from the front, back, top, bottom and sides of the four-engine B-17 prompted its nickname, the "Flying Fortress." A "Fortress Master Log" compiled by Dave Osborne says Boeing delivered the plane to Tulsa, October 14, 1942. It was transferred to Chelveston, England, in February 1943.

On days a mission was planned, the airmen would be awakened in the early morning hours and fed a hearty breakfast followed by a briefing describing the mission. They would then be taken to their planes and await the signal to take off. Once aloft, brightly colored "lead-ships" would direct the bombers to predetermined points where they would organize themselves into their attack formations.

The aircraft was unheated and open to the outside air. The crew wore electrically heated suits and heavy gloves that provided some protection against temperatures that could dip to 60 degrees below zero. They also wore flight jackets like that of Bud Wilschke.

Above 10,000 feet the crew donned oxygen masks as the planes continued to climb to an operational level that could be as high as 29,000 feet. Nearing the target, each man would put on a 30-pound flak suit and a steel helmet designed to protect against antiaircraft fire. Parachutes were too bulky to be worn all the time but crewmen did wear a harness that allowed them to quickly clip on their parachute when needed.

Bud Wilschke was a bombardier. "A bombardier sits right in the plexiglass nose of a Fort, so he sees everything neatly laid out in front of him, like a living-room rug. It seemed to me at first that I'd simply moved in on a wonderful show. I got over feeling sick, there was so much to watch . . . "

Airmen didn't always fly in the same aircraft each mission. Newer crew members were often be paired with more experienced pilots. Bud Wilschke's first three missions were April 17 with the Lester Personeus crew in *Hangar Queen*, May 4, with the same crew in *Nora II* and May 14 with A. P. Walker's crew in *Hangar Queen*.

On May 17, 1943, the 8th Air Force sent 159 bombers to attack the U-Boat pens and port facilities at Lorient and 118 planes bombed the target. One plane returned damaged beyond repair and 27 were damaged. Six planes were lost. Casualties that day were one killed, eight wounded, and 57 missing in action.

Bombed extensively by British and American air forces, in 1943–1944, the Lorient vicinity was nearly razed to the ground. However, despite being hit with 4,000 tons of bombs, the ingeniously massive German submarine pens at the harbor were not disabled. The structures still stand in 2020.

The intensity and immediacy of the ordeal of having their B-17 fall from the skies was captured in the reports that Bud and his buddy Bob Neil filed afterwards:

From Bud's MIS-X report, filed on return to England:

The 159 Forts flew in close formation, with enough space to reduce their vulnerability to attack. While crossing the Brittany coast, his plane developed engine trouble and lagged behind the rest of the formation. The propeller on #4 engine had to be feathered. They dropped down and back a bit.

The Fort was attacked by German Anti-Aircraft Defense FW 190s and badly damaged. The intercom was knocked out so the two pilots in the cockpit had no way of knowing the extent of the damage to plane or injuries to crew. With the glycol system on fire the aircraft was filling with fumes and it was difficult to see anything.

After dropping their bombs and leaving the target, the crippled Fort was again attacked by German fighters. The engines were hit and enemy fire riddled the plane. One engine after another was lost and finally pilot Indiere sounded the bailout bell.

During the precipitous descent, radioman Bob Neil passed out. Somehow, he bailed out (one of the others pushed him out and pulled his ripcord). Other crew members bailed out the nose hatch at 27,000 feet, over Auray, on France's western coast, Southern Brittany. Six were killed. Two died due to malfunctioning parachutes and one body was found shot through the head. Those who went down with the plane were navigator Roy Richards, top turret gunner John McFarland, ball gunner Walter Schenk, right waist gunner Dennis Cullinan Jr., left waist John D. Norris, and tail gunner Henry A. Mitchell.

From Bob Neil's handwritten account:

Robert Neil 1943.

"May 17th. After radio briefing, I checked my 50 cal. machine gun. We were using chest parachutes at that time. Mine was missing. So, I borrowed a backpack. As it turned out, this parachute saved my life. As I was putting out a fire in the bomb bay, I believe the airplane blew up. We were at 27,000 feet. Then every system was on fire and I blacked out. I believe the B-17 then blew apart. I fell approximately 15,000 feet, came to and opened my chute. Had my regular chest pack been on the plane I would not have had the time to snap it on."

French Helpers

Often having to quickly vacate their hiding place to avoid discovery or capture, Bud and Bob rarely found out what had happened to their helpers afterward.

Immediately after the war ended, French citizens who could prove that they had helped American airmen escape and avoid capture could apply to the U.S. government for monetary compensation. Letters and application forms were submitted to U.S. authorities based in France. From these documents it was determined if the applicant were eligible, and if so, how much the award would be. Those declassified records provide useful historical framework for understanding the events of the war and the operations of the French underground and Resistance. Bud estimated there had been over 25 people or families who had helped him and Bob. Records are often inconclusive but research now supports there were over 40. The following is a sample of a few of his helper's stories.

Mathurin Diabat—Ploemel

After Bud left Diabat's farm the day after the crash, the local Gestapo unit arrested Diabat, age 46, and threatened him with death or prison. His children reported having had guns held to their heads to force Diabat to talk. He was eventually released and allowed to return to his family. Although the documents in his National Archives file list James Wilschke on the application, they indicate compensation was refused with no explanation for the denial.

Robert Monin—Saint Julien de Vouvantes

Monin, 37, was betrayed and arrested shortly after sheltering Bud and Bob for one night at his home. He was sentenced to death but spared and deported to a concentration camp. A recipient of the Medal of Freedom, he survived internment and wrote to Bob Neil after the war.

Mme. Marie Moquet

Mme. Moquet helped many flyers and Resistance workers in her home, the Manoir de la Chaussée, providing a place for a doctor and nurses to care for the wounded.

In August 1944, just outside her property, Nazi troops disguised their tanks with American flags to cross the River Vilaine bridge, which was being guarded by French Resistance fighters. The fighters let down their guard and cheered the disguised Nazi tanks and were overwhelmed.

Six Resistance fighters were executed. After being forced to bury the bodies of the others, Célestin Poulain, the Manoir's loyal gardener, was stood against the garden wall and executed for possessing a gun and not revealing the property's hiding places. A plaque in the garden marks the spot of his execution and burial.

Mlle. Andrée Récipon

Not long after the Mass of the Maquis, Récipon arranged for Bud Wilschke and Bob Neil to be moved further along on their

Mlle. Récipon recieves honors from General deGaulle 1950.

exhausting journey. Because she knew the Gestapo were watching her every move, she did not reveal to the next helpers who she was or where the two airmen had originated. In November 1943, herself betrayed, she fled to Paris. Even while in hiding, Récipon continued her resistance work until the end of the war. Returning to her estate in Laillé, she established a nursing facility for victims of concentration and POW camps. After the war, Mlle. Récipon was awarded the French War Cross, the Medal of the French Resistance, the Military Medal, the French Medal of Freedom, and was made a Knight of the Legion of Honor. Today, a permanent stone altar has replaced the wooden one Bud and Bob built, a memorial and site of pilgrimage for friends of the Récipon family, who still live on the estate.

Félix Jouan—Bédée

On January 14, 1944, Jouan was transporting supplies on the way back from a mission to send a small group of aviators across the channel. A German military police patrol decided that his license plate was too soiled to read and not in compliance with Nazi regulations. They gave Jouan a scolding, made him clean off the plate and pay a fine, and he began to drive off.

As the van started to move away, an officer shined his flashlight inside, spying several black suitcases. The van sputtered and died, giving the soldiers an easy opportunity to capture him. Jouan was quickly seized.

Inside the suitcases were illegal radios used to communicate among Resistance cells and a cache of weapons. Another Resistance member traveling with him, Aristide Sicot, managed to escape and warn other Resistance members of the danger. Jouan was sent to Neuengamme and then Sandbostel concentration camps in Germany.

Ill with typhus, Jouan died shortly after liberation on May 29, 1945. Regarded as a hero in his hometown, he was honored by the village of Bédée with a street named for him, *Rue Félix Jouan*. He was awarded the Medal of Freedom by the American government and a memorial plaque describing his courageous feats was placed in the town square.

A photograph of Jouan with Bud and Bob at the farm is featured at the Bédée war memorial, *Monument aux Morts*. This image of the three men, smiling, wearing berets, their arms around each other's shoulders, has been featured on the cover of a book used by the city of Bédée to represent the area. Bud visited Jouan's daughter Annick during his 1983 return.

Noël Brédoux—Nantes

Noël Brédoux was born on Christmas Day, 1919. He was a 23-year-old mechanic and known trafficker in the summer of 1943. He worked for his dad, a blacksmith and mechanic who serviced cars, farm equipment and motorcycles in the small village of Guenrouet, northeast of Nantes. Noël owned a 202 Peugeot and Grand Sport Talbot automobiles and three motorcycles (all of which were confiscated by the Gestapo). His access to transportation made it possible for him to travel around the countryside, delivering food to American airmen. He also was able to create replicas of official seals to make false ID papers. His "authentic" papers allowed him to buy gasoline and freedom to travel by car.

Brédoux also did a brisk business in the black market, trading often with the occupying Germans and with his fellow citizens.

Brédoux smuggled Bud Wilschke and Bob Neil to Nantes, delivering them to Jeanne and Mimi Sébastien. Brédoux worked with Jean Chanvrin from May to September 1943. He was then betrayed by Chanvrin, who had been an informant for the Nazis.

Brédoux was arrested but managed to escape and flee Nantes. He was recaptured in December and deported to Buchenwald concentration camp in Germany. He survived and was liberated by

American forces April 11, 1945. He returned to Nantes and was honored by the U.S. with the Medal of Freedom and a monetary reward for helping Neil, Wilschke, and others. He immigrated to Canada but returned to France in 1960. He protested the Franco-German reconciliation movement and was outspoken at a ceremony to honor the dead, angering the local municipality. He was a spokesperson for the Resistance and never forgave the Germans.

Jean Chanvrin—Nantes

Jean Chanvrin met Noël Brédoux in May or June 1942. Through Brédoux he met the Sébastiens and others assisting Allied airmen.

The Neil family correspondence collection includes a neatly handwritten letter from M. Jean Chanvrin, dated August 17, 1947, sent from the Struthof Camp in Rothau, France. Chanvrin recounted how he "fetched" and sheltered Neil and his friend for "some weeks in my house." Shortly after, he and his parents were arrested by the Gestapo. Reportedly to secure his parents' release, Jean turned Nazi informant.

When Nantes was liberated in 1944, he was imprisoned by the French government. Chanvrin was convicted and condemned to death but his sentence was commuted to life. Chanvrin's letter claimed he had been blackmailed into his betrayal, and implored Bob Neil to write and confirm that he helped and hid them, to clear his name and help him be released from prison. It is not known if Bob Neil replied to Chanvrin, who was paroled in 1953.

Jeanne and Francine Sébastien—Nantes

Jeanne Sébastien and her teenage daughter, Francine, hid the Americans for about a week. Shortly after Bud and Bob left to head north to stay with Mme. Moquet at the Manoir de la Chaussée, the Sébastiens were betrayed to the Gestapo. They were deported to Ravensbrück, the notorious women's concentration camp in northern Germany. Francine was brought back to Paris, tried, and sentenced to death. On the eve of the liberation of Paris, the Swedish Consulate secured her release. She was brought to Sweden with other prisoners.

While the owners were under deportation, the Sébastien home was pillaged and destroyed at great loss to them. After the war, citizens who had helped American airmen could be given financial compensation. The U.S. provided 60,000 francs to the Sébastiens for their aid to Bud, Bob and other Allied flyers. Both were given citations and the Medal of Freedom from the United States government.

Archive documents confirm that it was "Jean Chanvrin" (who wrote Bob Neil from prison) who was the informant/enemy double agent who betrayed the women.

Abbé Held

One of Mlle. Récipon's guests at the Château de'Laillé was the Assistant Archbishop of Strasbourg, Abbé Held. He was hunted by the Gestapo after resisting their attempt to teach National Socialism in the Catholic schools of Strasbourg, Alsace. Abbe Held loved proving the Germans foolish, tricking them into giving him multiple identification cards. Shedding his clerical clothing and dressing as a lay teacher, he led a group of boys in an escape from Alsace into France to keep them from being recruited into the Hitler Youth. As they approached the border, he told the sentries that he was leading the boys on a training march to prepare them for German military service. Each time another question came, the boys saluted with a hearty *Heil Hitler!* And, fearing any disrespect to the Fuhrer, the German soldiers waved them through.

Once at the Château de'Laillé, Held posed as Father Patier, a visiting priest, which allowed him to move relatively freely. The local parish priest, Father Pierre Jegu, sheltered him in his rectory and later spent six months in a prison for it. Held stayed through most of the rest of the occupation, but an informant betrayed Mme. Récipon, and Held fled the Chateau, finding himself in Nantes during a bombardment. A blast threw him out of a window and buried him under rubble. He later crossed the Pyrenees and spent a brief time in a Spanish prison. At the end of the war he served as chaplain on a battleship.

M. Eugène and Mme. Germaine Langlet - Tulle

The Langlets provided Bud and Bob shelter in Tulle on two separate stays. After the Americans escaped the October '43 raid at the Langlet home, M. Langlet was arrested, interrogated and sent to a concentration camp, but survived. Robert Neil's correspondence collection includes a letter from Langlet, written in September 1945, describing his arrest and imprisonment.

Dear Comrade,
It is with a great pleasure I learned by Captain Gruber, of your success arriving in England. I was very worried about your fate since the evening we were forced to flee. The precaution was good because the very same evening of our departure, the Gestapo came to arrest me.

I did not have the pleasure to see and cooperate with the landing because I was deported in Germany. My only joy was to see your glorious squadrons who would bomb the boche, and each explosion filled me with joy.

I will not talk about the suffering in those Nazi camps, what is important is that we got them (the Nazis) and we hope that victory will bring fruits more beautiful than the last war and we will finally live in peace. My daughter wanted to write you in English, I hope you'll be able to read it and she would be happy that you respond to her in English.

I leave you, my dear comrade, shaking cordially your hand, my family sends you her good memory.
E. Langlet
M. Mme. Langlet
Rue de Nancy
Nantes Loire inférieure

[Sauvet letter] Pierre Sauvet letter to Bud 1983

Jean Villeroux

Villeroux was deputy to the mayor of Rivesaltes, and worked for Jean Olibo, the general secretary of the town hall. He sheltered Bud and Bob for eight days and helped them get to the escape line. He was a member of the Cotre and Brutus networks. Villeroux was arrested on July 22, 1944, after which he escaped and joined the *Maquis* until the end of the war. He died on November 8, 1966. In 1983, Bud again met Paulette Villeroux, his widow, at one of the reunion events.

Buddies

During World War II, dedicated people put themselves at risk for things they believed in. Bud and Bob were among those. So were the many helpers that stood up to danger to help them along their

Bud and Rosemary Wilschke.

Bud's jacket and Jim Wilschke Jr.

way. People relied on each other and lived up to the trust placed in them. They suffered long separations to serve honorably. It has been a privilege to learn of these brave humanitarians and tell their stories.

Bud and Rosemary had a favorite song that captured their feelings about each other, "My Buddy."

Life is a book that we study,
Some of its leaves bring a sigh,
There it was written, my buddy,
That we must part, you and I.

Nights are long since you went away,
I think about you all through the day,
My buddy, my buddy, no buddy quite so true.
Miss your voice, the touch of your hand,
Just long to know that you understand,
My buddy, my buddy, your buddy misses you

Buddies through all the gay days,
Buddies when something went wrong;
I wait alone through the gray days,
Missing your smile and your song.
Nights are long since you went away,
I think about you all through the day,

My buddy, my buddy, no buddy quite so true.
Miss your voice, the touch of your hand,
Just long to know that you understand,
My buddy, my buddy, your buddy misses you

Donaldson and Kahn, sung by Bing Crosby.

Sources and Acknowledgements

This book is based entirely on diaries, letters, newspaper articles, and other documented resources. Conversations and dialog were imagined based on factual sources.

Discovering and describing the details of this inspiring story would not have been possible without the generous support and encouragement of the Wilschke and Neil families. Many people in the United States and in France deserve acknowledgement and thanks for their contributions. Apologies to those we have missed.

> *Jeanne, James Jr., Sue, David, and Carole Wilschke*
> *Nancy Wilschke*
> *Linda Neil Lescault and John R. Neil*
> *Special French contributors:*
> *Mme. Cendrine Rodrigues*
> *Mme. Elise Bassereau*
> *Mme. Alice Diabat Jacob*
> *M. Jean Gautier*
> *Mme. Simone Brion*
> *M. Jean-Yves Thoraval*
> *M. Armel LeFloch*

Major material sources:

James S. Wilschke personal letters and papers collection

Robert G. Neil personal letters and papers collection

MIS-X Top Secret Reports 267 & 268 (Escape & Evasion declassified), 11/15/1943

An American Relives His 6 Months of 'Maquis' in Brittany, 1983 (newspaper article; translated from French)

A Wartime Log, by Art and Lee Beltrone, 1995

Clipped Wings, by O. M. Chiesl, 1948

Journey Underground, by David Prosser, 1945

Chicago Tribune, Chicago Daily News 1944 -Newspaper articles

Providence Journal 1944 -Newspaper articles

Ouest 1944—French newspaper articles

WWII Escape Lines Memorial Society,
    http://www.ww2escapelines.co.uk/

WWII Escape and Evasion Information Exchange, Keith Janes
    www.conscript-heroes.com/
They Came from Burgundy, by Keith Janes, 2017
Can Do Notes, Vol. 2 #2
Air Force Escape and Evasion Society Newsletter, March 2002
SOE in France, by M. R. D. Foot, 2004
305th BG and 8th Air Force Historical Society Facebook Groups
Aeroscout Research, by Chris Coffman, 2010
Steven Quillman, USAF/FB researcher
Find-a-Grave.com and Ancestry.com
War Eagles, Joe Boyle Oral History thesis, by Michael Norwood
    Mcdowell, 2005
Doug Thompson, Curator, Military Museum of Minnesota
*Hitler's Gateway to the Atlantic: German Naval Bases in France
    1940-1945,* by Lars Hellwinkel
Kate Wells, Reference Librarian, Providence Rhode Island
    Public Library
June Dunning, Reference Librarian, Mt. Vernon, Indiana
    Public Library
Red Lake Falls Gazette
Iowa State Historical Society
United States National Archives (helper files)
Sim Smiley, National Archives researcher
Krista Reynen, Chicago researcher
Bangor Maine Public Library
The Loft Literary Center, Lisa Bullard ("Start with the crash")
Brec'h Crash Site Memorial:
    http://www.aerosteles.net/steleen-brech-b17
Tales from a Tin Can: The USS DALE from Pearl Harbor to Tokyo Bay
    by Michael Keith Olson, 2007

The families of the crew:
Leslie Boyle Shipps and Joseph Boyle Jr.
Aaron Pelesasa and the family of Henry A. Mitchell, Jr.
Debbie Clarke (niece of John McFarland)
Dana Winfield (niece of Walter Schenk)
William A. Norris, *Liberal Opinions,* 2016 (younger brother of
    John Norris)
Dennis Timothy Rizutto, (great nephew of Dennis Cullinan)

Special thanks:

Col. Don Patton and the Harold C. Deutsch WWII History
    Round Table
Harrison Wojcik, for ongoing support and encouragement
Lillian Wojcik, editorial reader and cover design
Blake Foster, editorial reader
Stephanie Wolkin, editorial reader and French consultant
Dave Engel, sure-footed editor

Special thanks to my family and friends who patiently listened and supported my sometimes-dogged obsession with researching this story. Marla Okner and Lee Burtman, fellow story researchers and writers, you were so helpful in giving feedback and advice.

I want to especially recognize and thank my husband Jim, who worked alongside me and jumped in when I was unable to marshal my strength and focus to see this through to completion. I could not have done this without you.

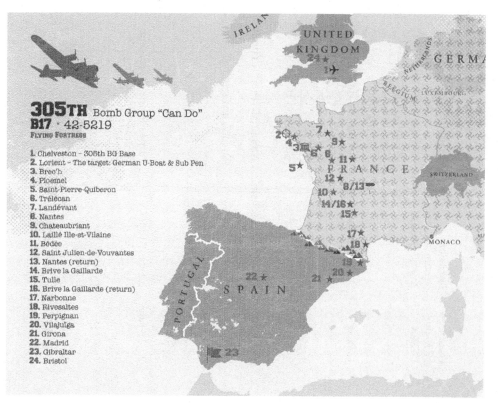

305TH Bomb Group "Can Do"
B17 · 42-5219
FLYING FORTRESS

1. Chelveston – 305th BG Base
2. Lorient – The target: German U-Boat & Sub Pen
3. Breo'h
4. Ploemel
5. Saint-Pierre-Quiberon
6. Trélecan
7. Landévant
8. Nantes
9. Chateaubriant
10. Laillé Ille-et-Vilaine
11. Bédée
12. Saint Julien-de-Vouvantes
13. Nantes (return)
14. Brive la Gaillarde
15. Tulle
16. Brive la Gaillarde (return)
17. Narbonne
18. Rivesaltes
19. Perpignan
20. Vilajulga
21. Girona
22. Madrid
23. Gibraltar
24. Bristol

Wilschke/Neil Timetable—1943

Date	Location	Primary Helpers	Notes/sources
17 May	Brec'h		Crash site (8 mi. from Ploemel) JSW
17 May	Auray/Ploemel	André Diabat, Michel Bertrand, Pierre Sauvet, Mme. LeBayon (Dupot/Dubot?)	JSW - parachuted into Diabat's farm field. Hid at Diabat's farm. RGN—parachuted into a meadow, 1 night on the run until a farmer took him in, made him shave his moustache.
18 May	St. Pierre-Quiberon	Valentin LeMouroux, Mme. LeChat	Met up with Bob Neil, then transported to an abandoned beach house; recuperated for 3 weeks.
8–19 June	Camors and Le Petit Roscoet	François Carlach Adrien and Henriette Joannic	Carlach transported the men hidden in an oxen-drawn cart. A Nazi soldier hitched a ride.
To 23 July	Trelecan/Landevant Pluvigner	Antoine Dreano & family / Dreano arrested and imprisoned, but was	Hid them in their house, and then the small chapel ("they killed a German" May '44. M. released.) JSW/RGN collections.
	Morbihan to Nantes	M. Noël Bredoux	Transported them to Nantes. Betrayed by Jean Chanvrin. Arrested Dec. 1943. Deported to Buchenwald. Survived.
20–26 July	Nantes (*Nont*)	Mme. Jeanne & Francine "Mimi" Sébastien	Hid the men 3 days. Betrayed by Jean Chanvrin. Arrested and deported to Ravensbruck camp. Survived.
1 week?	Langon (*Long-oo*)	Quentin Bocherel, Marie-Luce Moquet	Hid in a fishing shack along a towpath, then a hotel, then the Manoir de la Chaussée. While at the fishing shack, they were fishing with their host when a group of Nazi soldiers showed up to go swimming. They were able to move away. (JSW notes, JYT notes)
26 July to	Guémené-Penfao		

Date	Place	People	Notes
3-6 AUG		Mme. Durand – ? note from J-Y (no documentation)	
6–20 Aug	Laillé	André Recipon (Fr. Held, Marian Wilke)	Stayed at the Château de'Laillé, witnessed bombing of Rennes 8/8, helped build the altar in the woods. 1st Mass AUG 12th. JSW collection.
20 Aug 1 week–	Bédée (BED-ee)	Félix Jouan, baker/miller Annick (daughter) Marcel (son) being released from prison camp	While the men hid in the barn loft, a local Nazi unit pulled up and commandeered the barn for their head quarters. Joan captured Jan. '44 and died shortly after at the end of the war. Marcel too.
	Rennes (Renn)	André and Mme. Heurtier	Hosted the men one afternoon before they were driven to Châteaubriant
	Châteaubriant	Pierre Troudec, Marcel Letertre Bernard DuBois (from J-Y)	Letters in RGN collection; notes from Jean-Yves.
	Saint Julien de Vouvantes	Robert Monin	Spent one night at this man's family home. He was later arrested and sent to a concentration camp. RGN
Sept, up to and including 16 & 23	Nantes (return)	M. and Mme. Langlet Jean Chauvrin (informant) Pierre Mauge Jean Ligonday	Arrested and imprisoned after the war. While here, the men witnessed 3 bombing raids on Nantes
To 9 Oct	Nantes	Suzanne Clement	"Your mother in France" - RGN

Date	Place	Helpers / People	Notes
9–13 Oct	Brive/ Tulle/Brive	M. and Mme. Langlet— also helped the men in Tulle (houses in Nantes and Tulle) city.	Arrived by train. stayed a week or two with various farmers in vicinity of Brive. Tulle: escaped out the back door during a Nazi house-to-house search of the
13 Oct–7 Nov	Narbonne		Brive: a farmer agreed to buy them tickets to Narbonne and make sure they got on the right train. Began walking south towards the border; walked through a German firing practice range
7-17 NOV	Rivesaltes/Perpignan	Jean Olibo, M. Esteve Opoul. Rougier (all listed on Nat. Archives helper documents for Villeroux) Jean and Paulette Villeroux	The mayor's assistant Villeroux and his wife helped the men get to Perpignan and meet up with a group preparing to hike over the mountains. The group included US airman David Prosser, who in '45 wrote a book about the experience "Journey Underground"
15–17 Nov	Pyrenees		Led by a Spanish guide, 2 nights of hiking
17 Nov they tried to buy tickets	Vilajuïga, Spain		First town they came to. Arrested at the train station as
	Figueres, Spain Castle Saint Fernando		to Madrid. Held here 3 weeks with other political prisoners at http://www.castillosanfernando.org/en/
13 Dec	Madrid	US Embassy—Special Orders	Travel approved to Gibraltar
28 Dec	England	Sent cable to Rosemary	

Memorabilia

THEIR SIGHTS ARE TRAINED ON HAPPINESS—Lt. James S. Wilschke, bombardier, reported missing in action over Europe for seven months, was back home today happily reunited with his fiancee, Rosemary Crandall. [by a staff photographer.]

Their sights are trained on happiness.

A war story.

A War Story; A Love Story; A Good Story!

DAILY NEWS 1/4/44

(Picture on page 1.)

Rosemary Crandall's seven-month vigil of hope and faith that her fiance, Lt. James S. Wilschke, 23, a bombardier who has been reported missing over Europe since May 17, would come back has been rewarded. In a cable received yesterday at the home of her parents, Mr. and Mrs. Harry Crandall, 8034 S. Woodlawn av., the long-lost airman said "Okay to plan wedding now—maybe February."

The pretty 21-year-old secretary is going ahead with those plans. She is going to be a traditional bride, she said, and will have three bridesmaids.

Date Waits on New Cable.

She will be married at St. Francis De Paula Church. The date, however, cannot be set until Lt. Wilschke cables or writes more information on his homecoming.

A previous cable that he was safe was received by Miss Crandall last week, and another went to his mother, Mrs. Mabel Wilschke, 8017 Ridgeland av. "It was the first word we had received from him in more than seven months," his mother said, "but I never gave up hope. I placed him in God's hands and I know that the prayers of all his friends have brought him back."

Although the families have no information, it is presumed he may have escaped from a prison camp.

Met at Hirsch School.

Wilschke and Miss Crandall met at Hirsch High School, from which both graduated. He was graduated from the American College of Physical Education in June, 1941, and enlisted in the Army Air Forces six months later. He was commissioned a bombardier at Victorville, Calif., in October, 1942, and went overseas in February, 1943.

Miss Crandall was graduated from Wilson Junior College in June, 1941.

War hero returns.

THE CHICAGO SUN

SECOND SECTION   MONDAY, JANUARY 17, 1944   ★ PAGE 15

OL BUDGET ASKS 13,000

AIR HERO RETURNS TO GET HIS GIRL

Lt. James Wilschke and his bride, the former Rosemary | year-old bombardier, had to bail out over enemy territory
Crandall, just after their wedding Saturday at St. Francis | in Europe last May and was missing for seven months. He
De Paula Church, 78th and Dobson sts. Lt. Wilschke, 23- | finally worked his way through enemy lines back to Britain

May 8, 2017 ceremony, Brech. —

From left: Travis Bejlovec, Denise Wilschke, Jim Wilschke Jr., Sue WilschkeVaughan, Barbara Wojcik, Scott Vaughan, Carole Wilschke, Leslie Crandell, Katie Bejlovec, Lillie Wojcik, Jim Wojcik.

From left: Scott Vaughan, Sue WilschkeVaughan, Travis Bejlovec, Katie Bejlovec, Barbara Wojcik, Jim Wojcik, Carole Wilschke, Leslie Crandell, Denise Wilschke, Lillie Wojcik, Jim Wilschke Jr.

Barbara Wojcik, 2017.

Made in the USA
Coppell, TX
25 September 2021